U.S. History: People and Events 1607–1865

Author: George Lee
Consultants: Schyrlet Cameron and Suzanne Myers
Editor: Mary Dieterich
Proofreaders: Cindy Neisen and Margaret Brown

ISBN 978-1-62223-643-5

Printing No. CD-404264

Mark Twain Media, Inc., Publishers
Distributed by Carson-Dellosa Publishing LLC

Table of Contents

Introduction

When studying history, students are surrounded by informational text. They must have the ability to understand its purpose, gather key ideas and details, make inferences, and evaluate the information. The goal of this book is twofold: to help students learn about important people and events in U.S. history and to practice informational text comprehension skills.

There are 42 lessons in *U.S. History: People and Events 1607–1865.* Each lesson includes a reading selection and an activity. Each lesson can be used independently or can be combined with other lessons into a unit of study.

Reading Selections

Decisions—we make them all the time. However, we don't usually think of them as being important; in fact, many are not. But the consequences of our decisions can be far-reaching. Decisions made by one person often affect others as well. Some decisions have affected not only individuals and those with whom they come in contact but have changed history. Most of the time, the person making the decision was thinking about himself or herself and what was to his or her advantage at that moment. He or she was not thinking in terms of how people hundreds of years from then would react to it. Some decisions turn out for the better, some for the worse. At times, there were surprising side effects. Eli Whitney's cotton gin is a good example. He was not thinking about how it would create a new demand for slaves. He was only interested in helping farmers clean seeds from their cotton.

As students read the selections, they need to realize that people of the past were products of their time and place, just as we are. We may not approve of things they did, but we cannot judge them by the standards of our time. We can't imagine any intelligent person thinking slaveholding is fine, so we assume they must have felt guilty for owning human property. However, if they grew up in the South before the Civil War, slavery was part of their society, and they may never have met a person who opposed slavery. No one asked what slaves wanted, but eventually some African-American men and women made decisions affecting themselves and history. Fighting duels was another sign of the times, but it wasn't much different than the death-defying risks some people take today. The role of women was much more restricted than in the modern world. Men thought that women were there to cook, tend the garden, and produce children. They thought it was a waste of time to educate women or listen to them. As a result, a woman's role was very limited in making major decisions that affected the nation. Nevertheless, some women made or began making major historical breakthroughs.

Reading Activities

The activities in *U.S. History: People and Events 1607–1865* evaluate and extend the reader's comprehension by:

1. promoting thoughtful consideration of the text;
2. supporting the reader's comprehension with online experiences;
3. checking the reader's comprehension;
4. extending the reader's understanding of the text;
5. identifying the influence or impact of an event;
6. analyzing and explaining the relationship between people, events, and ideas;
7. analyzing primary and secondary sources; and
8. integrating visual information (i.e., photos, maps) with text.

Introduction (cont.)

Reading Comprehension Skills

Reading comprehension refers to a wide range of skills readers use to get meaning from text. While these skills develop over time, the activities in this book provide practice and reinforcement in the following skills:

- stating central idea
- stating main ideas
- identifying supporting details
- citing textual evidence
- making inferences
- following directions
- locating references
- recalling information
- summarizing or paraphrasing ideas
- recognizing text features
- determining word meaning
- identifying text structures
- distinguishing facts from opinions
- conducting research
- categorizing information
- identifying cause and effect
- making comparisons
- identifying the 5 W's

U.S. History: People and Events 1607–1865 has been correlated to Common Core State Standards and other current state, national, and Canadian provincial standards. Visit www.carsondellosa.com to search and view its correlations.

Time Line

We tell the story of our lives by dates. Dates also help us understand history. By dates, we can look at the past and see the order in which events occurred. They also help us keep historical events in sequence. This time line covers events from 1492 to 1865.

1492 Christopher Columbus sails to New World
1585 Roanoke Island Colony established, disappears by 1591
1607 Jamestown Colony established in Virginia
1619 First African slaves arrive in Jamestown
1620 Plymouth Colony established by Pilgrims
1624 New Netherland Colony established
1630 Massachusetts Bay Colony established
1664 New Netherland renamed New York
1676 Bacon's Rebellion
1682 La Salle claims Louisiana for France
1692 Salem Witchcraft Trials
1754–1763 French and Indian War
1756–1763 Seven Years' War in Europe
1763–1766 Pontiac's Rebellion
1763 Proclamation Line drawn
1764 Sugar Act
1765 Stamp Act
1766 Stamp Act repealed
1767 Townshend Duties
1770 Boston Massacre
1773 Tea Act; Boston Tea Party
1774 Intolerable Acts
1775 Battles of Lexington and Concord; First Continental Congress; Battle of Bunker Hill
1776 Second Continental Congress; Declaration of Independence; Battle of Trenton
1777 Battle of Princeton; Battle of Saratoga; French Alliance
1781 Articles of Confederation; Battle of Yorktown
1783 Treaty of Paris
1785 Land Ordinance divides Northwest Territory
1786 Shays' Rebellion
1787 Northwest Ordinance; Constitutional Convention
1788 Constitution ratified
1789 Washington inaugurated; French Revolution
1791 Bill of Rights ratified
1793 Cotton gin invented
1794 Whiskey Rebellion
1795 Battle of Fallen Timbers; Jay's Treaty
1796 Adams elected president
1797 XYZ Affair
1798 Alien and Sedition Acts

Time Line (cont.)

1800	Jefferson elected president
1803	Louisiana Purchase; *Marbury v. Madison*
1804–1806	Lewis and Clark Expedition
1807	*Chesapeake* Affair; Embargo Act
1811	Battle of Tippecanoe
1812	War of 1812
1813	Battle of Lake Erie
1814	Treaty of Ghent ends the War of 1812
1815	Battle of New Orleans
1816	Second Bank of the United States chartered
1820	Missouri Compromise
1821	Adams-Onis Treaty
1822	Santa Fe trade opens
1823	Monroe Doctrine
1825	Erie Canal
1828	Jackson elected president
1830	Webster-Hayne debate; Indian Removal Act
1831	Nat Turner's Rebellion
1836	Texas War for Independence
1837	Panic of 1837
1841	First wagon trains to Oregon and California
1844	James K. Polk elected president
1845	Texas annexed
1846–1848	Mexican-American War
1846	Wilmot Proviso
1849	California Gold Rush
1850	Compromise of 1850
1854	Kansas-Nebraska Act; Republican Party formed
1857	*Dred Scott* decision; Panic of 1857
1859	Harpers Ferry Raid
1860	Abraham Lincoln elected president; South Carolina secedes
1861	Fort Sumter bombarded; Lincoln calls for 75,000 volunteers; Battle of Bull Run
1862	Battles at Shiloh, Second Bull Run, Antietam; Pacific Railroad Act; Homestead Act
1863	Emancipation Proclamation; Battles of Vicksburg and Gettysburg
1864	Lincoln reelected
1865	Robert E. Lee surrenders at Appomattox Court House; Lincoln assassinated; Thirteenth Amendment ratified

Queen Isabella and Christopher Columbus

Queen Isabella of Spain studied the face of the sailor who stood before her. He seemed self-assured, experienced, and certainly bold, but was he insane for what he wanted to do, and would she be wise to back him?

Queen Isabella

In 1492, Isabella was 41 years old and had already proven herself as a woman who knew what she wanted. Born into the royal family of Castile, her family had tried to marry her off twice while she was very young. One prospective husband died when she was 10; the other died on his way to their wedding when she was 15. In 1469, she married the man she chose, Ferdinand of Aragon, and together they began to conquer the rest of Spain. She knew the look in the sailor's eyes—that desire to achieve and conquer shone in her eyes as well. Her advisors told her the sailor was doomed to failure. Ships were not strong enough, and Asia was too far away.

Christopher Columbus

Christopher Columbus, a sailor, was also 41 years old. He came from a humble Italian family of weavers. He had been drawn to the sea at an early age. When he was 15, the ship on which he sailed was attacked by pirates, and he landed in Portugal. There he learned valuable skills: reading, writing, navigation, and seamanship. In 1479, he married and for a time worked as a merchant. He also sailed in the Atlantic, where he learned and practiced the skills needed for open ocean sailing. He traveled on voyages to the Canary Islands and Africa's Gold Coast, where he learned about trade winds. These voyages would give him valuable experience.

Christopher Columbus

To Columbus, it seemed logical to assume that one could reach China by sailing west, and the treasures of the Orient would enrich the person and nation that was first to arrive. Most educated people knew the world was round; that wasn't the problem. The question was whether the ships of the time, caravels, could make such a long journey. Columbus tried to persuade the rulers of Portugal, Spain, and then England to sponsor the trip, but all rejected him. Again, he returned to Spain where the war to remove the Moslems from Grenada was ending. Again, the queen turned him down, so he started to leave for Portugal. But a messenger caught up with him and told him to return to the palace. The queen had decided in his favor; he would be given the title "Admiral of the Ocean Seas" and would receive ten percent of the revenues from anything he found. In a dramatic gesture, she said she would sell her jewels if necessary to fund the trip, but money was raised elsewhere. With three small ships, Columbus set sail in August 1492.

Columbus discovered a small island, now known as Hispaniola, on October 12, 1492, and assumed he was somewhere near India. For that reason, he called the friendly Taino natives on the island "Indians." He would make four voyages all together but proved to be a better explorer than ruler. There were many complaints about his using natives as slaves and the harsh way in which he and his family ruled. In 1499, he was taken to Spain in chains. Later his title and money were restored. Queen Isabella died in 1504; Columbus died in 1506. To his dying day, Columbus was sure his discoveries were on the outskirts of China.

Name: ______________________________ Date: ____________________

Queen Isabella and Christopher Columbus: Activity

Directions: Complete the graphic organizer. Cite evidence from the selection to support your answer.

What experiences prepared Christopher Columbus to become the "Admiral of the Ocean Seas"?

Experience 1

Experience 2

Experience 3

Experience 4

Captain John Smith and Jamestown

Other nations besides Spain were interested in establishing colonies, especially after Cortes conquered the Aztecs of Mexico and Pizarro the Incas of Peru. In both cases, they took large quantities of gold from the natives. Portuguese sailors moved down the coast of Africa, and their ships came back with gold, ivory, and slaves. England was also interested, but their explorer, John Cabot, found no great wealth, and only a few Englishmen were interested in colonizing. Sir Humphrey Gilbert tried to establish a colony in Newfoundland in 1583, but he died at sea, and the settlers returned after a cold winter. In 1587, Sir Walter Raleigh sent 117 settlers to Roanoke Island (North Carolina), but this colony disappeared.

The London Company

Establishing colonies was too expensive for any one person to afford. A new system developed: the joint stock company. Groups of people would each put up part of the cost and receive a share of the profits. The Muscovy Company traded in Russia and the East India Company in India. In 1606, the London Company was formed, and it sent 144 settlers to develop a coastal settlement at Jamestown in Virginia. One of those men was 27-year-old John Smith.

John Smith

Smith's motto was *Vincere est vivere,* "to conquer is to live." He had been tossed overboard from a sinking ship and had fought the Turks. The Turks captured him and held him as a slave with a chain around his neck. He escaped and finally returned to England in 1604. When he learned about the expedition to create a new colony, he signed on. He was supposed to be a member of the council for the colony, but after arguing with the ship's captain, Smith finished the voyage in chains. Smith was released after a jury trial.

In December 1607, Smith was captured by Chief Powhatan, but his daughter, Pocahontas, risked her life to save his. When he returned to Jamestown, he was arrested and charged with causing the deaths of the two men who had gone with him into Powhatan territory. After he was found not guilty, he was elected council president.

Starving Times

The Jamestown colony was in danger of starvation, despite the fact that the soil was good and plenty of food could be found. Six-foot-long sturgeon swam in the ocean. Deer were abundant, and turkeys weighing 70 pounds were nearby. But the men who came were looking for quick riches, so they wandered up and down the beaches looking for gold nuggets. They wanted to get rich and go home. They ignored the danger they were in. Smith ordered that every man must work or would receive no food. The colonists began to grow blisters on their hands as they tilled fields and built houses. After Smith was injured by a gunpowder explosion, he returned to England in 1609. He later returned to North America, and in 1614, he drew maps of a region he named "New England." In 1615, while exploring the New England area, he was captured by French pirates. He escaped and finally reached England in 1616. He spent the rest of his life quietly writing books about his adventures.

What Were the Results?

Later leaders of Virginia would continue to force settlers to work. The London Company never made any money from their efforts, but John Rolfe, who was married to Pocahontas, took a local plant, tobacco, and exported it to England.

Name: ______________________________ Date: ____________________

Captain John Smith and Jamestown: Activity

A **motto** is a phrase that expresses the beliefs or ideals guiding an individual, family, or institution.

Directions: Complete the graphic organizer by describing three events from the reading selection that support the idea that John Smith's motto was a guiding force in his life.

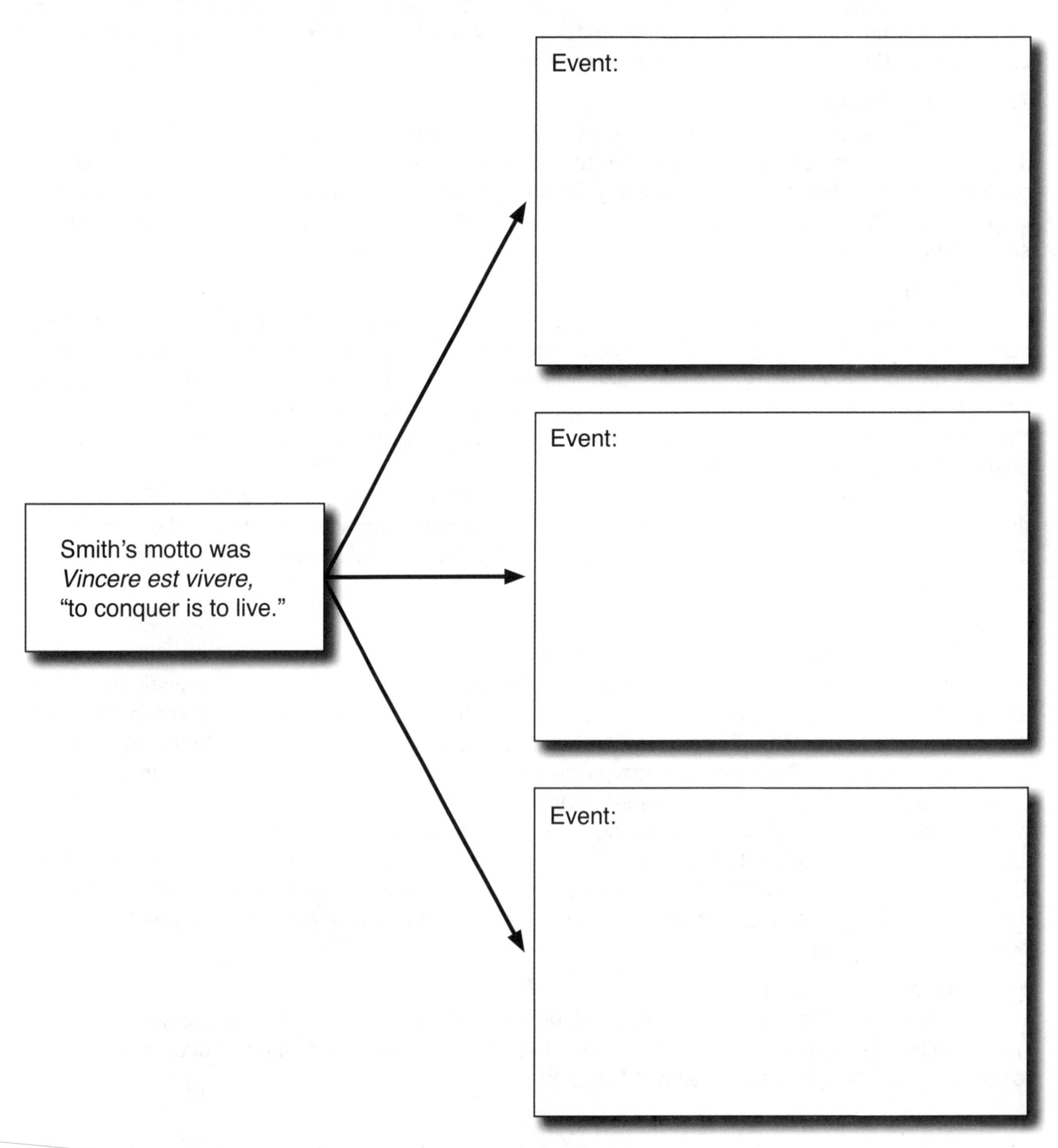

The Pilgrims and the Puritans

Puritans and Separatists

When Henry VIII created the Church of England (Anglican), many of his people were unhappy. Catholics did not like the king assuming the power of the pope, but the greatest problem came from citizens who felt the new church was too similar to the Catholic Church. One group was called "Puritans" because they wanted to "purify" the church and remove statues, bishops, and rituals. Another group went even further—they wanted to separate from the Anglican church and were known as "Separatists." Both groups followed the teachings of John Calvin, who stressed strict obedience to the Ten Commandments. They also believed that God would punish nations that did not follow Him. Therefore, they would not obey those leaders, even if they were kings. They would rather die than surrender to laws they believed to be immoral.

Both Puritans and Separatists found life under the Stuart rulers who came after Elizabeth I especially hard. The Stuarts were too much like the Catholics, as far as they were concerned. Because of their opposition, these religious groups faced beatings, brandings, loss of property, and even death. They longed for the day when they would be able to practice religion in their own way. Eventually in 1630, the Puritans would leave England and settle the Massachusetts Bay Colony in America.

The Pilgrims

In 1608, a group of Separatists called Pilgrims went to Holland, which was more tolerant of their views. However, the only jobs they could get were as day laborers, and their children grew up more Dutch than English. Rather than return to England to live, they made a deal with the London Company. The merchants would pay for their trip to North America; after seven years, they and the company would divide the profits.

The captain of their ship, the *Mayflower,* took them to the coast of Massachusetts. The ship lay anchor at the spot they named "Plymouth," the name of the port in England from which they had sailed. However, they had landed north of the London Company's territory, so they had no legal authority to the land they claimed. Many of the settlers were not Pilgrims, including their military commander, Miles Standish, so their religion could not be the bond holding them together. They feared attacks by Native Americans, the French, and the Spanish. Their situation required that everyone conform to certain rules of conduct. They knew that either they worked together or all would die.

The Mayflower Compact

An agreement known as the Mayflower Compact was drawn up and was signed by 41 men on November 11, 1620. They agreed to form a civil body and to abide by the "just and equal laws" that would be passed. Despite able leadership from William Bradford, the colony remained poor and small until it was absorbed by the Massachusetts Bay Colony in 1691. Plymouth's greatest contribution to history may have been the Mayflower Compact. By agreeing to accept the rule of the majority and by putting it into written form, Plymouth's settlers set a precedent for written constitutions that would follow.

Name: ______________________________ Date: ____________________

The Pilgrims and the Puritans: Activity

Direction: Use information from the reading selection to complete each activity.

Activity 1

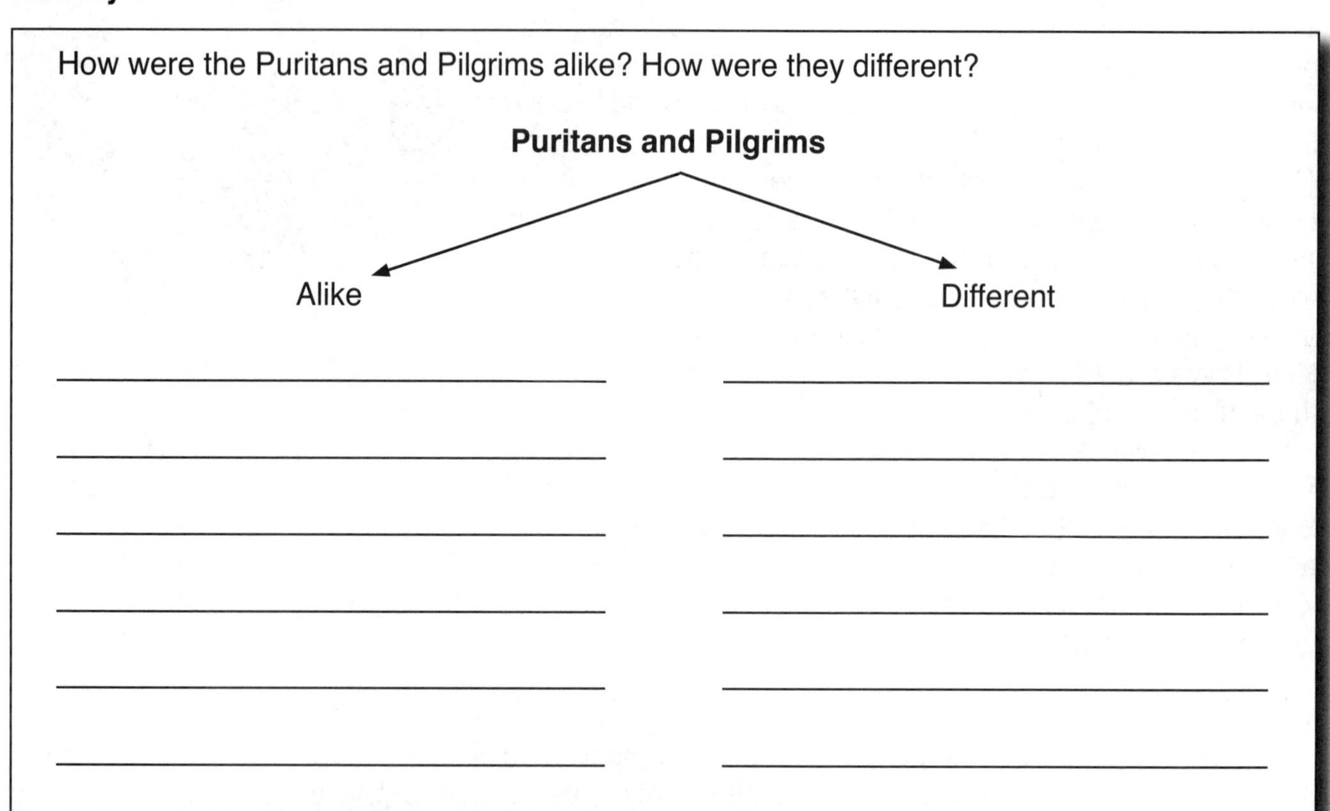

Activity 2

Explain what the author meant by the statement, "Plymouth's greatest contribution to history may have been the Mayflower Compact." Cite evidence from the reading selection to support your answer.

The French and Indian War Begins

Colonizing America

England, France, and Spain were like three boxers with long memories of past battles. When they weren't fighting, they were preparing for the next match. Many who left those countries and came to America wanted to forget the past, but as long as they were colonists, they could not. They were part of a greater empire, and when rulers declared war, the shockwaves would reach them.

To the north of the British colonies was New France (Canada); French Louisiana lay west of the Mississippi River. To the south was Spain's colony, Florida. All three nations saw the importance of having Native American allies. The Algonquins supported the French, the Iroquois backed the English, and Spain's allies were the Seminoles and Creeks. When war came, the nations would recruit their Native American allies to join their army as scouts and warriors.

In Europe, wars were fought by professional soldiers. When a king needed more trained men, he often rented them from another ruler who was not fighting. The two armies met in an open field, moved to within about fifty yards of each other, and fired volleys in unison. They did not fight in the winter or in bad weather. In America, it was much different. Battles were smaller and might be fought in any type of weather by untrained farmers, fur traders, fishermen, or craftsmen under leaders they elected.

Washington and the French and Indian War

When George Washington was a boy, his older brother Lawrence taught him the basics of soldiering. George Washington became a militia officer and surveyor on the side, but most of his time was spent running the large farm he owned at Mt. Vernon on the Potomac River. Two wars had been fought in North America before Washington was born, and one ended while he was in his early teens. These involved raids on small frontier communities. Young Washington took part in the French and Indian War.

The Ohio River Valley was claimed by both France and the colony of Virginia. In 1754, the governor of the colony of Virginia learned the French were building a string of forts in the upper Ohio River Valley. The governor sent Washington to inform the French they had to leave the area. After the French refused, the governor sent Colonel Washington, then 21, and a small army of 150 men to force the French to leave. Washington chose a low place in the woods to build Fort Necessity. The French attacked the fort. Colonel Washington and his men were outnumbered. Also during the battle, a heavy rainstorm flooded the fort and soaked all the gunpowder. Washington and his men were forced to surrender. This battle is considered to be the beginning of the French and Indian War.

In July of 1755, British soldiers and Virginia militia recruits led by General Edward Braddock tried to force the French out by marching to attack the French at Fort Duquesne. Braddock wanted to fight as they did in Europe with the soldiers lined up in rows, marching close to each other. Washington tried to change his mind about this, but the general would not listen. When they were deep into the forest and about 10 miles from the fort, the French soldiers and their Native American allies attacked. The British soldiers dressed in red uniforms and marching in rows made themselves easy targets. Terrorized by war whoops and an invisible enemy concealed behind trees in the thick forest, Braddock's troops scattered and ran. Braddock was wounded, and the British retreated. On July 13th, Braddock died from his wounds.

Washington now had experience in battle and found it exciting. He also learned that fighting in America required different tactics because of its geography and its people. The war ended in 1763 with the signing of the Treaty of Paris.

Name: ______________________ Date: ______________

The French and Indian War Begins: Activity

Directions: Complete the graphic organizer. Support your reasons with evidence from the reading selection.

Reason:

Reason:

Why didn't the European system of fighting a war work in America?

Reason:

Reason:

New Laws Anger Colonists

Navigation Acts

The end of the French and Indian War brought great relief to the American colonists. The French no longer threatened them from Canada. As English subjects, they were proud of their country and themselves for their role in the war. At times, English policy had bothered them. They did not like the Navigation Acts that controlled colonial trade and authorized the collection of taxes in the colonies on non-English imports. Since these laws had never been enforced before the war, colonists rarely thought about them.

James Otis

Writs of Assistance

The government tried to stop smuggling with search warrants called writs of assistance. These would allow any government official to search any home looking for anything. At that time, a Bostonian named James Otis worked for the government as a lawyer, and if anyone protested the search, it would be his job to defend the law. Rather than do that, he resigned and went to court to argue *against* the writs. He lost his case, but many colonists began to see that liberty was in danger of being lost. John Adams wrote later: "Then and there the child Independence was born."

After the Seven Years' War in Europe, England was badly in debt and felt that, since their American colonies had gained the most from the war, the colonists should pay part of the cost of sending an army to protect the frontier from Native American attack. English leaders never considered how colonists might react. To them, colonists were like children, and the English were the parents. Anything the king and Parliament decided was something the American colonies must do.

Acts of Parliament

In 1765, Parliament passed the Stamp Act. It required that a revenue stamp be placed on legal documents, newspapers, and marriage licenses. They also passed the Quartering Act, which said the colonists would have to provide housing for 10,000 British soldiers who would be sent to protect them. The colonists did not like taxes, and they did not want the soldiers.

Again, Otis was on his feet complaining, but this time, others were with him. Patrick Henry told the Virginia legislature that colonists had every right that Englishmen had, and one of the most important English rights was that citizens could not be taxed without representation. He said the only people who could tax in their colony were Virginians.

In the Massachusetts legislature, Otis called for a meeting of the colonies to take place in October 1765. Nine colonies sent delegates to the meeting. They said they were loyal to the king and admitted that Parliament had the right to pass laws for the colonies. However, they stated that only the colonial legislature could tax the people. On the streets, groups of men and boys calling themselves Sons of Liberty destroyed stamps and threatened those who had been appointed as stamp agents. Protests by colonists and a change of leadership in Parliament caused the Stamp Act to be repealed. Colonists cheered when they heard the good news. They paid no attention to a law called the Declaratory Act passed at the same time, which said that England had every right to make any law for the colonies that they chose. This would lead to future trouble.

Name: ______________________________ Date: ____________________

New Laws Anger Colonists: Activity

Directions: Complete the chart with information from the reading selection.

English Law	Summary of Law	Colonists' Reaction
Navigation Acts		
Writs of Assistance		
Stamp Act		
Quartering Act		
Declaratory Act		

Sam Adams—Rabble Rouser

Tax on Imports

After the Stamp Act controversy, relations with England never got back to normal. In 1766, Charles Townshend became Chancellor of the Exchequer (treasurer) of England. The next year, he persuaded Parliament to pass the Townshend Acts. These laws taxed American imports of lead, paper, glass, and tea. Money from the tax would pay the salaries of British officials in America. In the past, legislatures had paid their salaries and used paychecks as a way to control the governors. Americans protested again and stopped buying British goods (a boycott). The men chosen as tax collectors knew they were unpopular, and those in Boston were protected by two regiments of Redcoats (British soldiers).

Sam Adams

Redcoats on American soil were unpopular, and Sam Adams, a colonist, used that to turn molehills into mountains. He would not rest until America was independent and there were neither British soldiers nor officials on American soil.

Adams was a Harvard graduate, smart in studies, but terrible in business. He took over his father's business, and it went broke. He became Boston's tax collector and didn't collect the taxes. By the time he was 42 years old, his hair was gray, he dressed poorly, and he had very little money. There was one thing he did well—he stirred up the public against the British. Since he was poor, he needed and got the financial support of the wealthy shipowner John Hancock. When James Otis became ill, Sam Adams was appointed the anti-British leader.

Boston Massacre

In 1770, a British soldier on guard duty was pelted with snowballs, and other British soldiers came to his rescue. A mob gathered around them; one soldier was knocked down and another hit with a cane. The soldiers fired and killed four civilians. Sam Adams called it the "Boston Massacre" and persuaded a silversmith, Paul Revere, to make an engraving of it so people could not only read about it but see it.

Tax on Tea

The American boycott was successful, and Parliament once again backed down—but not completely. In 1770, they repealed all the Townshend duties except the tax on tea. In 1773, Parliament passed a law that gave the East India Company a monopoly on tea trade. The only legal tea was that imported by the East India Company; however, the company sold directly to the customer. American merchants who sold smuggled tea did not like that and stirred opposition to the tea tax as a way to get public support behind them.

When Sam Adams learned that tea ships had arrived in Boston, he organized an unusual protest. He and his friends (the Sons of Liberty) dressed in costumes like Mohawks and dumped 342 chests of tea into the harbor. Some Americans approved of this, but others, like Benjamin Franklin and George Washington, did not. If England had not reacted as it did, it might have been a soon-forgotten act of vandalism, but George III made it an important event.

Intolerable Acts

The English overreacted, and in 1774, Parliament passed a series of laws known in America as the Intolerable Acts (Coercive Acts in England). They closed the port of Boston, put Massachusetts under a military governor, and housed troops in private homes. Americans united as never before against these laws. If England could treat one colony that way, all were in danger of losing their freedom.

Name: ______________________________ Date: ______________________________

Sam Adams—Rabble Rouser: Activity

Directions: Complete the graphic organizer by listing an effect for each event. Support your answers with details from the reading selection.

Event		Effect
Event 1 In 1766, Charles Townshend became Chancellor of the Exchequer of England.	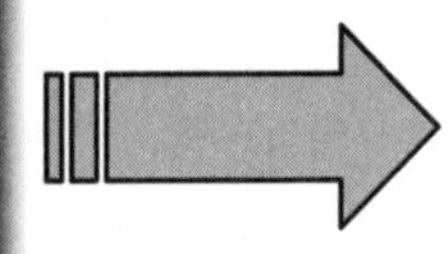	
Event 2 In 1770, a British soldier on guard duty was pelted with snowballs.	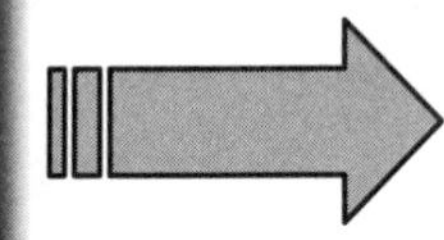	
Event 3 In 1773, Parliament passed a law that gave the East India Company a monopoly on tea trade.	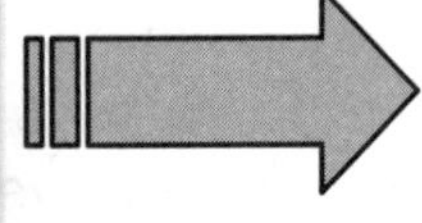	
Event 4 In 1774, the English passed a series of laws known in America as the Intolerable Acts.	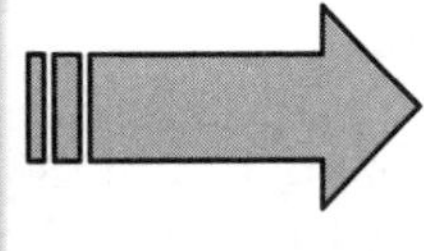	

Patrick Henry

Americans were outraged when they learned Parliament had passed the Intolerable Acts. It was unreasonable that a whole colony be punished for the actions of a few men. If England could do this to Massachusetts, what would prevent the same thing happening to any other colony that offended the king? Protest was heard now in other parts of British America, but the most eloquent was by Virginia's Patrick Henry.

His Life

The son of a tobacco farmer, Patrick Henry hated farm work as a boy, so his father gave him a store to run—it lost money. He got married at an early age, and his parents gave the new couple a farm, but the house burned. He tried running a store again, but once more he failed. He enjoyed reading and decided to become a lawyer. He barely made it past the bar examination, but he was popular and soon had a thriving law practice. In 1763, he took a case involving a minister's pay and turned it into an attack on the king. His opposition called this treason, but the audience was in his hands.

In 1765, he was elected to Virginia's House of Burgesses. This was the year of the Stamp Act, and no one doubted his opinion on that subject. He gave a speech proposing five resolutions to protect the rights of the colonists of Virginia and advocating resistance to King George III and Parliament. The exact words of his speech were not documented, but witnesses related that he compared King George III to the tyrants Julius Caesar and King Charles I. Accused of treason, Henry responded, "If this be treason, make the most of it." When the resolutions passed, he left public office and returned to his law practice for a time. In 1774 when word reached Virginia of the Intolerable Acts, Henry could not sit idly by while freedom was in danger. He was pleased to be chosen as a member of the First Continental Congress, which met in Philadelphia.

Quick Fact

In 1955, the U.S. Postal Service issued a $1 postage stamp honoring Patrick Henry.

Continental Congress Meets

Most delegates were not as outspoken against England as were Sam Adams and Patrick Henry. Adams had been advised not to mention the word "independence," for fear it would only scare off Southern delegates, so he sat quietly and let Patrick Henry do the speaking. Henry proclaimed, "The distinctions between Virginians, Pennsylvanians, New Yorkers, and New Englanders are no more. I am not a Virginian, but an American." A resolution was passed declaring the Coercive Acts unconstitutional, but there was no demand for independence.

When General Thomas Gage arrived in Boston with an army, Governor Dunmore of Virginia feared the worst from men like Henry and barred the doors to the House of Burgesses. The legislators met in Richmond, and Henry gave his most famous speech. He said the time for patience was over, that every effort to persuade the king had failed, and closed with, "Is life so dear or peace so sweet as to be purchased at the price of chains and slavery? Forbid it, Almighty God. I know not what course others may take, but as for me, give me liberty or give me death!"

What Were the Results?

Henry's words had a force to them that still affects people who feel their liberty is endangered. The memory of those words was to become useful in 1776 when debate began on whether or not to declare independence.

Name: ______________________ Date: ______________

Patrick Henry: Activity

Patrick Henry's words had a force to them that still affects people who feel their liberty is endangered.

Directions: Explain what Henry meant by the statements below. Use information from the reading selection to support your answers.

Statement	Explanation
Statement 1 *If this be treason, make the most of it.*	
Statement 2 *I am not a Virginian, but an American.*	
Statement 3 *Is life so dear or peace so sweet as to be purchased at the price of chains and slavery?*	
Statement 4 *I know not what course others may take, but as for me, give me liberty or give me death!*	

The Declaration of Independence

In June of 1774, British General Thomas Gage was appointed military governor of the Province of Massachusetts Bay. King George III instructed Gage to implement the Intolerable Acts and punish the colony for the Boston Tea Party.

First Continental Congress

In September of 1774, delegates from 12 of the colonies met in Philadelphia. The meeting became known as the First Continental Congress. Some delegates, who wanted to be loyal to England but also wanted to have more freedom, came up with ideas for developing a dominion status. That is, Parliament would have no control over them, but they would stay loyal to the king. The delegates sent a document to King George III demanding British troops be withdrawn and the rights of the colonists be restored. When the demands reached the king, he and Parliament agreed that the colonies were in a state of rebellion.

Battles of Lexington and Concord

British General Thomas Gage and the king's troops ruled in Boston, but outside the city, it was the Committee of Safety that was in charge. They were gathering guns and gunpowder, drilling their militia, and preparing for a showdown. Gage's spies told him about arms being collected at Lexington and Concord, Massachusetts, and he sent approximately 700 men to destroy the supplies. Paul Revere and William Dawes rode to warn the American colonists that the Redcoats were coming. Dawes escaped British patrols, but Revere was captured and held for a time.

On April 19, 1775, at Lexington and again at Concord, the militia faced the British, and after someone fired (no one is sure which side fired first), British volleys forced the inexperienced militia to leave in a hurry. The British soldiers found little in the way of ammunition or supplies to take, so they marched back to Boston. Americans, hidden behind rocks and trees, attacked them all the way. The British casualties included 73 men killed and 174 wounded.

Second Continental Congress

In May of 1775, tensions ran high in Boston, which was now surrounded by militia. The Second Continental Congress met again in Philadelphia. The decision to appoint George Washington to command the army was a big step toward separation, but delegates were still reluctant to face the big question: "Are the thirteen English colonies in North America prepared to break their historic ties to the greatest empire on Earth?" From that question came others. If we do try, can we win? Who might we persuade to help us? What will happen to those who sign a document declaring independence if the effort fails? The only question for which they knew the answer was the last. If they failed, the penalty for traitors included imprisonment, loss of fortune, and death.

On June 7, 1776, Richard Henry Lee of Virginia proposed a resolution stating, "That these united colonies are, and of right ought to be, free and independent states." This caused much debate, and many members had to wait for instructions from home before they could vote. On June 11, 1776, the Continental Congress asked a committee to draft a formal document explaining to the world the reasons for their actions. The committee included John Adams, Benjamin Franklin, and Thomas Jefferson. The others left Jefferson with the job of writing the Declaration of Independence.

The Declaration of Independence was adopted on July 4, 1776. As Benjamin Franklin stood in line to sign it, he commented, "We must all hang together, or assuredly we shall all hang separately." It was meant as humor, but there was a truth to it that the others all understood. To fail was to die, but honor and liberty were worth the risk.

Name: ______________________________ Date: ____________________

The Declaration of Independence: Activity

Directions: Use the events from the reading selection to create a time line. The first event is done for you.

Declaration of Independence Time Line

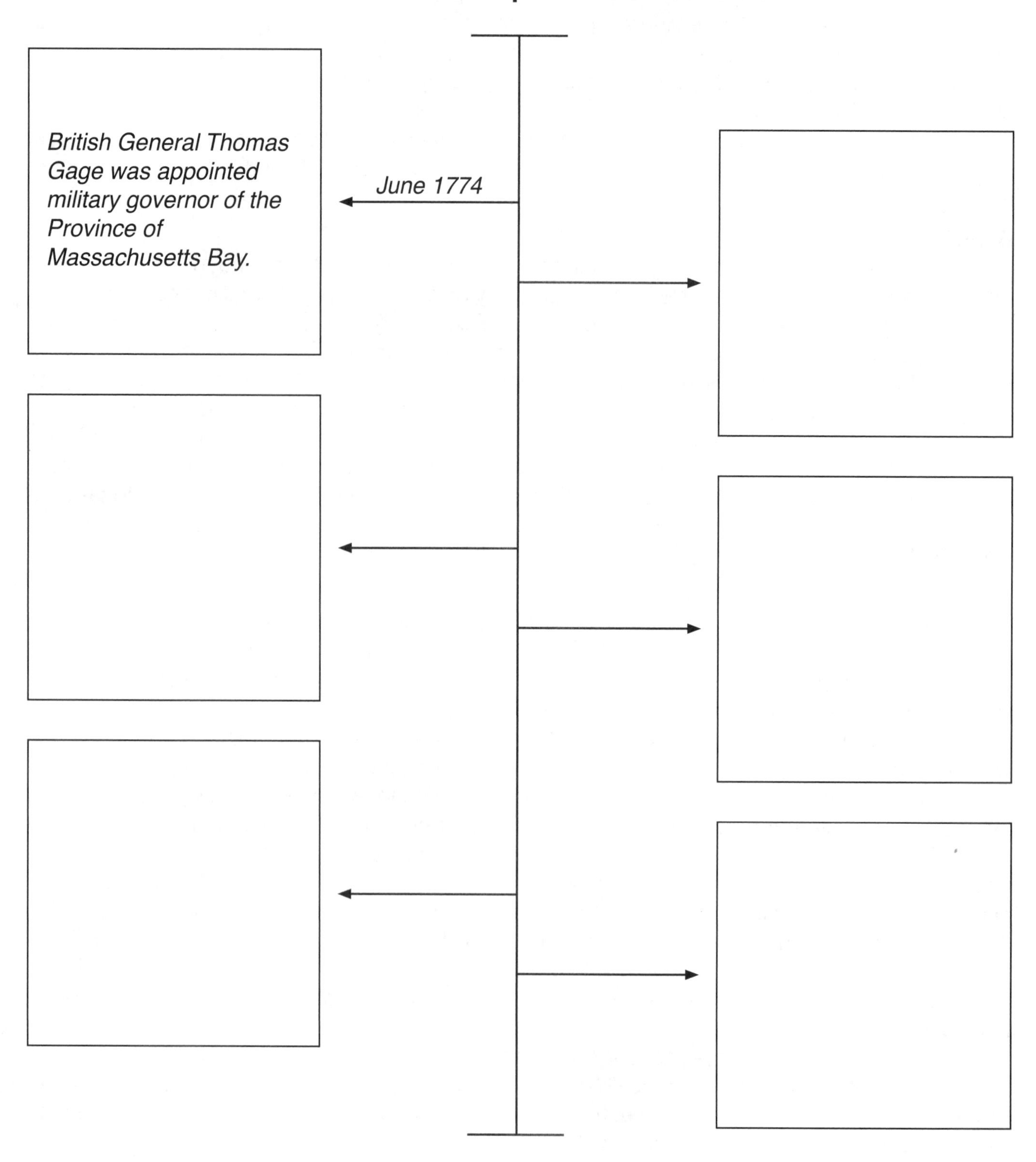

Americans Fight for Liberty

Battle of Bunker Hill

In the summer of 1775, General Thomas Gage had sent General William Howe's British soldiers to take the hill near Charlestown, Massachusetts, held by the militia. Three attempts were made before the Americans withdrew, but one-third of Howe's men were dead or wounded. Howe had expected an easy win, but the results shocked him. He was more careful after that.

> **Did You Know?**
>
> During the Battle of Bunker Hill, most of the fighting occurred on nearby Breed's Hill. As the Redcoats advanced, Colonel William Prescott, commander of the militia, reportedly told his men, "Don't fire until you see the whites of their eyes!"

Washington Takes Command

As Washington rode to Boston to take command of the 15,000 soldiers gathered there, a messenger informed him that a battle had taken place. Once in Boston, he organized his army. In battle, he would depend on the men recruited by Congress, the Continentals. They would be his "professionals." Since each colony had its own militia, he would use them as well, but he always feared they could not stand the pressure of battle. His officers were chosen by Congress, many for political reasons. His main problem was not the British army but getting the supplies he needed. The French secretly sent the Americans guns and ammunition, but there were other shortages as well: food, clothing, shelter, and pay for the men. Many soldiers deserted; Thomas Paine called them "sunshine patriots." Washington guessed the British would next target New York City. He stationed some soldiers on Long Island, the others on Manhattan.

British Defeat Washington's Army

Washington guessed right; General Howe landed on Long Island with 32,000 men, including 9,000 German professional soldiers. Since most of these were from Hesse, Americans called all the German soldiers Hessians. At Long Island, the Americans did not fight well, but a heavy rain came, so Washington was able to withdraw to Manhattan. While there, he was defeated again.

Victory at Trenton

In the winter of 1776, the British army was scattered in New York and New Jersey. So far, they had won all the battles, but Washington was still loose and dangerous. Knowing that German troops were at Trenton and were surely not expecting an attack in a snowstorm on Christmas Day, Washington's men crossed the Delaware River. A note was sent to the German colonel warning of a possible attack, but the note was written in English. Since he couldn't read English, he just put it inside his coat. The battle was swift, and 1,400 Germans were either killed or captured. Later, the note was read to the dying colonel.

What Were the Results?

Trenton was the beginning of a brighter day for Washington's army. The victory gave confidence to an army that had been trounced time after time. Many soldiers who had planned to leave decided to stay. New men joined the army.

Name: ______________________ Date: ______________

Americans Fight for Liberty: Activity

Directions: Use information from the reading selection to complete the page.

1. Place a check mark next to the text features used in the selection.

   ◯ title
   ◯ headings
   ◯ subheadings
   ◯ italicized print
   ◯ boldface print
   ◯ bullets
   ◯ photograph
   ◯ illustration
   ◯ diagram
   ◯ chart
   ◯ map
   ◯ sidebar
   ◯ caption

2. Place a check mark next to the organizational structure used in the selection.

   ◯ argument/support
   ◯ cause/effect
   ◯ chronological/sequential
   ◯ classification
   ◯ compare/contrast
   ◯ definition
   ◯ description

3. Place a check mark next to the author's purpose for writing the selection.

   ◯ to inform
   ◯ to entertain
   ◯ to persuade

4. List one opinion stated in the reading selection.

   ____

   ____

5. List three important facts you learned.

   A. ____

   B. ____

   C. ____

Benedict Arnold—Traitor

Benedict Arnold

Benedict Arnold's name was once listed among the most outstanding American officers. He had earned the trust of General Washington. And yet, today his name is often used as a synonym for *traitor.*

Early Military Career

Arnold joined the militia during the French and Indian War. At 21, he went to New Haven, Connecticut, and became a book salesman and pharmacist. When he learned of the Battle of Lexington, he got a colonel's commission. Together with Ethan Allen's Green Mountain Boys, he took Ft. Ticonderoga and its guns from the British. This was one of the first major victories for the colonies.

The Continental Army

After the battle at Ft. Ticonderoga, Arnold joined the Continental Army under George Washington. Arnold then led an unsuccessful expedition to capture Quebec City and received a bad leg wound during the attempt. When General Guy Carleton's English troops tried to move down Lake Champlain in 1776, Arnold blocked them. He was given the rank of brigadier general, but Congress criticized the fact that his books were not in order. The next February, five brigadier generals were promoted to major generals, but he was passed over. Washington demanded an explanation of why Arnold was overlooked for promotion and was told that Connecticut already had two major generals.

Washington persuaded Arnold to stay in the army. After he played a major role in stopping British officer "Barry" St. Leger's drive down the Mohawk Valley, Arnold joined General Gates' army at Saratoga. In the battle, Arnold led charges against Burgoyne's lines and received a thigh wound. Envious of Arnold's standing with General Washington, Gates did not mention Arnold in his official report of the battle.

Becoming a Spy

While Arnold was recovering from his wounds, Washington put him in charge at Philadelphia, where he fell in love with and married an English sympathizer, Peggy Shippen. His wife had more expensive tastes than he could afford, and he fell heavily into debt. In addition, Pennsylvania officials charged that he was using their militia as his personal servants. It was not hard for Arnold to excuse what he and Peggy now planned.

Secret discussions were held with British agents. Arnold was to persuade Washington to give him a command at West Point, an important position on the Hudson River, and then he would turn it over to the British. Washington was surprised when Arnold asked for West Point but gave in to his friend's request. Once at West Point, contact was made with a British spy, Major John Andre. They agreed that if Arnold could deliver West Point, he would receive £20,000 and a commission in the British Army. On his way south after the meeting, Andre was captured, and the secret papers were found inside his shoe. Arnold made a quick getaway, just before Washington arrived on an inspection tour.

When Washington was given evidence of what Arnold had done, he could hardly believe it at first, but he sent his men out to find him. Arnold was next seen leading Loyalist troops, and he escaped to England when the British army surrendered. His reputation was ruined; the British, like the Americans, saw him only as a traitor.

Name: ______________________________ Date: ______________________

Benedict Arnold—Traitor: Activity

Directions: Use information in the reading selection to help complete the graphic organizer.

Central Idea

Events in Benedict Arnold's life influenced his decision to betray his country.

Supporting Detail

Supporting Detail

Supporting Detail

Summary

Treaty of Paris

European Support for the War

A basic part of the colonists' strategy from the beginning of the war had been to win European support. America would need guns, gunpowder, and financial support. Since England had defeated Spain and France in previous wars, those countries naturally disliked England. Holland was a rival on the oceans and would also like England put in its place. The United States sent diplomats to Europe to encourage these countries to help America in its fight for independence. Benjamin Franklin was the key diplomat in France, John Jay in Spain, and John Adams in Holland. Of these, the best-known was Franklin.

Noted for his scientific discoveries, his inventions, and his words of wisdom in *Poor Richard's Almanack*, Franklin was adored by the French public. Since they saw Americans as backwoodsmen, Franklin started wearing a coonskin cap. Beyond the showmanship, there was purpose behind his actions. He got secret shipments of supplies, he talked to young officers eager to volunteer for the American army, and he arranged for the French to give secret grants and loans. At first, Count Vergennes, the French foreign minister, dared not give open support to the Americans; they might quit fighting, and England would have every excuse to pounce on France.

Treaties With France

The victory at Saratoga caused Count Vergennes to push the reluctant King Louis XVI to recognize the United States. In 1778, two treaties were signed; the first was a trade treaty, and the second was an alliance. Each side promised it would continue to fight until the war was won; neither would stop fighting without getting the permission of the other.

Preliminary Treaty of Peace Signed

The war was far from over when the agreements with France were signed, but English hopes were clearly fading. England was even offering self-rule within the British Empire. Their agents tried to bribe Benjamin Franklin and members of Congress to get them to agree to sell out the cause. When British agents approached Franklin, he told them the only terms acceptable would be: independence, British troops leaving American soil, and America gaining the right to fish off the Great Bank of Newfoundland. Franklin called in Jay and Adams to help with the work. Jay did not trust the French to put American interests above those of France. He suggested America make its own deal with England. Adams agreed with Jay, and the outnumbered Franklin gave in. A preliminary Treaty of Peace was signed in 1782.

> **Quick Fact**
>
> Adams, Franklin, and Jay signed their names to the Paris Treaty in alphabetical order.

Treaty of Paris

The problem was the Americans had violated their agreement with France that neither side would stop fighting without the consent of the other. Franklin was chosen to write the letter to Vergennes telling him what America had done. He explained that this was only a "preliminary" treaty and would not be binding until after France approved. In 1783, the Treaty of Paris was signed. It gave America independence and the region west to the Mississippi River. Florida was given back to Spain. Congress was to ask states to return the property of Loyalists (those supporting England) that had been seized by the states.

What Were the Results?

The colonial period was over. The United States of America was a proud new independent nation comprised of thirteen independent states.

Name: ______________________ Date: ______________

Treaty of Paris: Activity

Directions: Complete the graphic organizer by providing the impact of each event. Use information from the reading selection to support your answer.

Event		Impact
Event 1 Benjamin Franklin sent as America's key diplomat to France	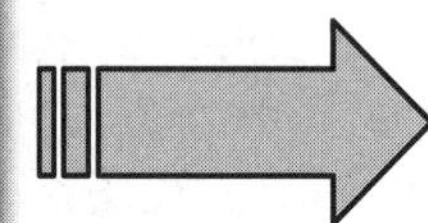	
 **Event 2** The victory of the Continental Army at Saratoga	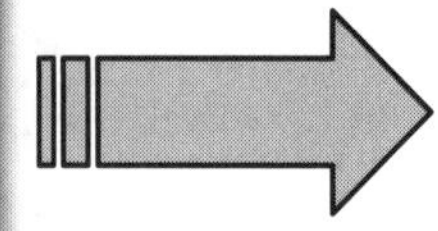	
Event 3 The United States signs a treaty of alliance with France	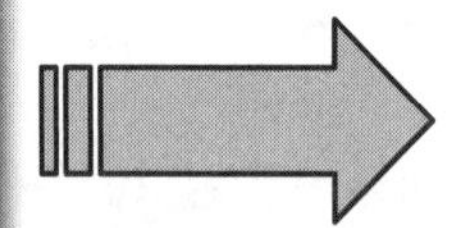	
Event 4 Treaty of Paris signed	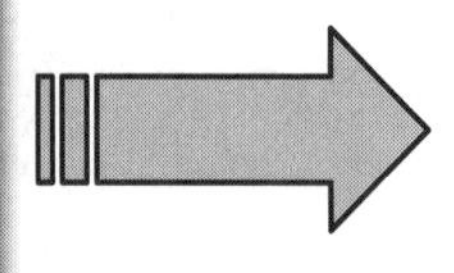	

Articles of Confederation

The States Form a Confederation

The Declaration of Independence was the beginning of a new era in America. The states were quick to throw off their status as colonies and began writing their constitutions. Remembering royal controls and appointed governors, they relied now on their legislatures to rule. However, there was also a war to fight, so the role of the Second Continental Congress was continued. The states made it very clear that they were in charge and had no intention of giving up any more power than necessary.

Congress had been like a committee called to deal with one problem, but it continued to meet because new problems kept coming. If they were to be permanent, however, their purpose needed to be better defined. John Dickinson of Delaware chaired the committee that drafted the Articles of Confederation, which were approved by Congress in November 1777. Careful to avoid any hint they were going to take power from the states, the new union was called a "league of friendship." Before the Articles could go into effect, all 13 states had to approve, and that was not easily done.

Small coastal states like Maryland fretted because other states had large land claims west of the mountains. Only after these states gave up their western land claims and turned them over to Congress did Maryland give approval for the Articles in 1781.

The Articles gave Congress the power to declare war and peace, manage foreign affairs, maintain an army and navy, issue and borrow money, and deal with the Native Americans. Each state, no matter how large or small, got one vote. Members of Congress were chosen by the state legislature for one-year terms. Nine votes were required before any policy could be adopted, and 13 votes were required before the Articles could be amended.

Weaknesses of the Articles

Many qualities necessary for a strong government were missing:

- There was no president or executive at the head.
- It had no power to tax; money was raised by begging it from the states and by borrowing.
- State support was needed but not received. States, when asked for money, often declined. Sometimes states failed to appoint delegates, and many times, there was no quorum in Congress.
- Members of Congress often did not take their responsibility seriously, and the public ignored them.
- Congress had no power to enforce the peace treaty after it was signed.
- The lack of unified control in America made the threat of foreign involvement more likely.
- Congress' inability to pay the army's back wages made the threat of a military takeover a possibility.

What Were the Results?

The Articles provided a temporary means for the states to work together through the Revolution, but a better approach was needed for the nation to survive. Two major pieces of legislation came out of the Confederation period. The Land Ordinance of 1785 provided a means for surveying western lands and dividing them into townships. The Northwest Ordinance of 1787 provided a system for governing the Old Northwest and creating new states.

Name: ______________________ Date: ______________________

Articles of Confederation: Activity

Directions: Use information from the reading selection to complete the graphic organizer.

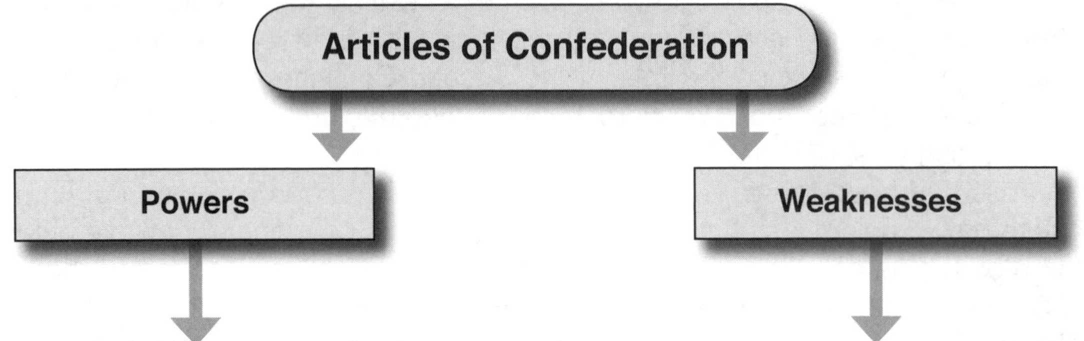

Details	Details

Old Soldiers Threaten Civilian Rule

Throughout the Revolutionary War, George Washington had more than just the English to contend with; he also had jealous officers who felt *they* should be in command, not him. Brigadier General Thomas Conway organized a plot against Washington during the war, but it backfired, and Conway was forced out of the army. More serious was the threat of General Horatio Gates, who made no secret of his feeling that he was the better general and should be leading the army.

Old Soldiers Become Restless and Angry

When the war ended, the soldiers returned to their shops and farms, but Congress had no money to pay their back wages. Their only currency, the "continentals," had been put out with great speed but without anything to back it. Those who had served their country were mostly poor men with families to support. In those days, there were debtors' prisons for people who did not pay their bills. As creditors pressured them to pay their debts, the old soldiers became restless.

Did You Know?

In 1976, George Washington posthumously received the title General of the Armies from the U.S military. This is the highest rank in the United States Armed Forces.

Anger with Congress was not easily solved. Toward the end of the war, Washington received warnings that discontent was strong, and some in the army had strong ambitions. At the military camp at Newburgh, New York, protest letters were being passed around, and a meeting of officers was arranged. It was assumed that Washington would not attend the meeting, but they were wrong. The general came to the front, tried to reassure them, and advised them to do nothing to stir up public discontent. He had accomplished nothing; the officers sat grim and determined. Then he remembered a letter he had received from a Congressman and pulled it out of his coat. He started to read, but the letters blurred in front of him. He reached in his pocket and pulled out eyeglasses. Few had ever seen him with glasses. He apologized, "Gentlemen, you will permit me to put on my spectacles, for I have not only grown gray, but almost blind in the service of my country." Many of the soldiers wept, and the meeting ended with the passing of a resolution expressing confidence in Congress.

Problems were far from over, however, as revolts by some state militias indicated. In Rhode Island, debtor farmers got control of the legislature and began to put out worthless paper money to pay off debts. The New Hampshire legislature was surrounded by mobs demanding cheap paper money; the militia came to their rescue.

Shays' Rebellion

The most serious trouble came in Massachusetts, where former captain Daniel Shays led a group of discontented poor farmers. They were angry when courts tried to seize their property because they couldn't pay their taxes. The rebellion was finally put down, but it was a warning of more trouble ahead unless a stronger government could be formed.

What Were the Results?

The Confederation was not capable of paying its soldiers or its debts. The threat that old soldiers might take over was real. Unless an answer came soon, the goal of freedom would be lost, not to a foreign king, but to leaders who might exploit the desperation of old soldiers.

Name: ______________________ Date: ______________

Old Soldiers Threaten Civilian Rule: Activity

Directions: Complete the graphic organizer with details from the reading selection.

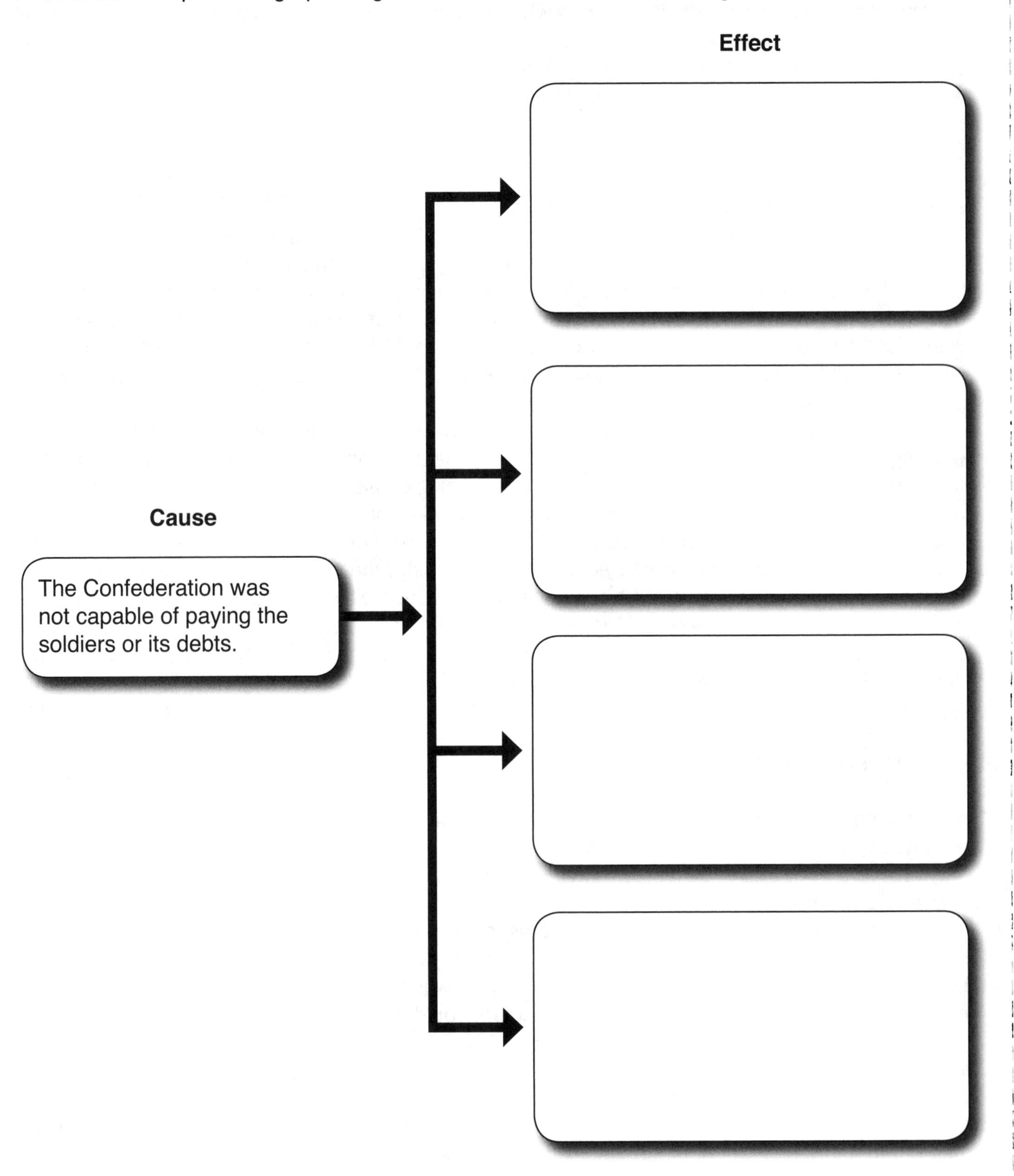

The Constitutional Convention

After retiring from the army, Washington wanted to spend the rest of his life in peace at home at Mount Vernon, but he kept getting disturbing information that could not be ignored. British forts were still standing on American soil; the French were demanding that the bankrupt Congress repay their loans, and Spanish agents were working among the Native Americans. The continental currency was a joke, and states were taxing imports from foreign countries and other states. This was leading to fierce arguments between states. Congress had little power under the Articles. Shays' Rebellion had demonstrated growing public disorder. Fear of a military takeover was always present. Unless something was done soon, everything Washington had fought for would be lost.

Meeting at Mount Vernon

In 1781, the thirteen states ratified the Articles of Confederation. Within the next few years, however, it became clear that this plan to rule the states had serious problems. In 1785, Virginia and Maryland delegates met at Mount Vernon to work out problems of trade on the Potomac River. The meeting went very well, so it was decided that another conference should take place the following year at Annapolis, with all 13 states invited.

Annapolis Convention

Only five states sent delegates to Annapolis to continue working on problems with trade among the states. Alexander Hamilton suggested that another meeting be held in Philadelphia in 1787 to consider changing defects in the Articles of Confederation. Congress gave a feeble endorsement to the proposal, and states were asked to choose delegates to go to the convention.

Constitutional Convention

At the time, Washington suffered from malaria and rheumatism, but when asked to go to the Constitutional Convention, he accepted. That news gave special meaning to the gathering, and states began to choose talented men for their delegations. The average delegate was in his early forties, although Ben Franklin, who was now 80 years old, raised that average. Most were college educated, had served in state legislatures or Congress, and were financially well off. Lawyers, merchants, and farmers were overly represented; no poor men, women, or minorities participated.

To no one's surprise, Washington was chosen president of the convention. The 55 delegates agreed not to try to fix the Articles of Confederation. Instead they decided to write a new constitution. They made an important early decision to keep the proceedings secret; compromising was easier if no one was giving headlines to the press. A few delegates, including James Madison, took notes on the debates. Later, these would be important to historians since the official minutes gave only a brief outline of what was said and decided.

Much compromising went on as delegates from large and small states, North and South, commercial and agricultural states, liberals and conservatives, struggled to find the words upon which they could agree. Fortunately, they all believed there should be three branches of government (legislative, executive, and judicial), and each should be independent of interference from the others. They believed in checks and balances, so each could stop the others from grabbing power. All believed in a republican form of government, one where supreme power rests with the people.

What Were the Results?

Out of this meeting came the Constitution of the United States, an incredible document that has served the nation for over 200 years and has only been amended 27 times.

Name: ______________________ Date: ______________

The Constitutional Convention: Activity

Directions: Use information from the reading selection to complete the graphic organizer. The first one is done for you.

Event	Year	Result
Congress approved the Declaration of Independence	1776	**Result** *The American colonies were now independent states.*
Articles of Confederation Ratified	1781	**Result**
Meeting at Mount Vernon	1785	**Result**
Annapolis Convention	1786	**Result**
Constitutional Convention	1787	**Result**

George Washington Becomes President

Despite his reputation as a general, George Washington much preferred a farm field to a battlefield or an inspection of his mules to a review of his troops. However, he could never be just a peaceful farmer again. When duty called, he answered. When the Constitutional Convention created the office of president, everyone there knew who would be chosen. The Electoral College unanimously chose him, and once again, Washington left his farm to serve his nation. He did not want the job and wrote that his feelings were like those of the criminal on the way to be executed.

Washington's Administration

Washington organized his administration around old and trusted friends: Alexander Hamilton was secretary of the treasury, Henry Knox was secretary of war, and Thomas Jefferson was secretary of state. In domestic affairs, the government would bring order to the chaos of the Confederation period. Hamilton's policies not only paid the government's bills, but paid the Confederation's and the state war debts. Federal taxes were levied and collected. When Western farmers rioted against the tax on whiskey, Washington sent militia units into the riot area, and order was restored. The ringleaders of the Whiskey Rebellion were arrested, but Washington pardoned them. He did not want to fill prisons; he just wanted Americans to obey the law.

Foreign Affairs

Most of Washington's concerns were in foreign affairs. In July 1789, a few months after Washington took the oath of office, the French Revolution broke out, and Americans were thrilled that the French had followed their example. French mobs beheaded noblemen, and in January 1793, they executed King Louis XVI and his wife. In February, France declared war on England. Federalists supported England, but Republicans favored the French. Washington knew that getting involved in this affair would be dangerous for the United States, so he issued a Proclamation of Neutrality. He warned that Americans helping either side would be punished. The new French minister (ambassador) arrived soon afterward. His name was Edmond Genet. He ignored Washington's policy by persuading Americans to raid English ships. After repeated warnings, Washington decided to expel Genet from the United States. Genet then reversed himself and begged for permission to stay.

The English captured American ships and forced American sailors to either join the British navy or they were sent to prisons with terrible conditions. Frontiersmen feared Native-American attacks as long as British forts existed on American soil. Washington asked Chief Justice John Jay to go to England and work out a treaty. The Jay Treaty (1795) only did part of what needed to be done. The English did promise to leave the forts, but other problems were left to be taken care of later. The treaty barely got the two-thirds approval of the Senate that the Constitution required. It passed 20-10.

Washington's Farewell Address

After eight years as president, Washington retired. Before he left office, he gave parting advice to the nation in his farewell address. He warned against forming political parties because they divided the people when national unity was required. He also warned against permanent alliances with other nations that might draw America into their wars.

Name: ______________________________ Date: ______________________

George Washington Becomes President: Activity

Directions: Read the statements about George Washington. Place a check mark on the line under F if the statement is a fact or under O if the statement is an opinion.

F **O**

_____ _____ 1. George Washington much preferred a farm field to a battlefield or an inspection of his mules to a review of his troops.

_____ _____ 2. When the Constitutional Convention created the office of president, everyone there knew who would be chosen.

_____ _____ 3. The Electoral College unanimously chose Washington as president.

_____ _____ 4. Washington left his farm to serve his nation.

_____ _____ 5. Washington did not want the job of being president.

_____ _____ 6. Most of Washington's concerns were in foreign affairs.

_____ _____ 7. In July 1789, a few months after Washington took the oath of office, the French Revolution broke out.

_____ _____ 8. French mobs began to cut off the heads of noblemen, and in January 1793, they executed King Louis XVI and his wife.

_____ _____ 9. Washington asked Chief Justice John Jay to go to England and work out a treaty.

_____ _____ 10. After eight years as president, Washington retired.

_____ _____ 11. Washington was a better general than he was a president.

_____ _____ 12. In his farewell address, Washington warned against forming political parties.

Eli Whitney Invents the Cotton Gin

Slavery was an unpopular institution by the 1790s. Northern states abolished slavery by court action or by laws they passed. Southerners had too much money invested in slaves to go that far, but they did make it easier for owners to free their slaves if they wished. The main use for slaves was tobacco production, but the crop was hard on the soil. Washington and many other people felt slavery would end someday because it was not profitable.

Eli Whtney

Eli Whitney was from New England; as a boy he liked to invent and repair things. He worked his way through Yale by fixing the college's equipment. A carpenter said to him, "There was one good mechanic spoiled when you went to college." He wanted to study law, but that required money he did not have, so he became a tutor on a Georgia plantation. There he overheard farmers discussing their problems. There were two varieties of cotton: upland and sea island. Of the two, sea island had the longest fibers and was the easiest to clean (to remove the seeds). However, it only grew in a limited area. Upland cotton would grow best in the South, but those pesky seeds were hard to untangle from the cotton boll. If only someone could devise a way to remove the seeds from cotton, the Southern farmer could become more productive.

Eli Whitney

Cotton Gin

Whitney began work on a machine. The timing was perfect because another man, whom Whitney did not know, was going to make his machine especially useful. The man was Samuel Slater, who had escaped from England with plans for a cotton mill sketched in his mind. Landing in Rhode Island, he and some other men built the first cotton mill in America in 1790. The combination of a product, the means to develop it, and a world market desiring it is a sure road to success.

Whitney's machine was called a "cotton gin." It was a box with a hand-cranked cylinder that fed the cotton through narrow slots wide enough for the cotton but too narrow for the seeds. The seeds dropped to the bottom and out of the way. When improvements were made to it, one person could do in a day what had taken months to do before. Whitney and his partner, Phineas Miller, patented their machine in 1794, but imitators quickly made copies of it. Whitney never made much money from that machine; however, he did get a government contract to produce muskets. To save costs, he used molds to make the same parts for each gun. It was the beginning of interchangeable parts, a system that makes mass production possible today.

What Were the Results?

In 1792, the United States produced 10,000 bales of cotton. By 1825, the year Whitney died, the cotton states produced 533,000 bales. Cotton products were far more popular than wool for clothing; and with the means to produce cotton cloth expanding, it was more affordable. There were also negative consequences. Expansion of cotton production required more workers, and that made a new market for slaves. The price of slaves shot up, and the South would never voluntarily surrender this large pool of workers.

Name: ______________________________ Date: ______________________

Eli Whitney Invents the Cotton Gin: Activity

Directions: What were the consequences of the invention of the cotton gin? Use evidence from the reading selection to support your answer.

Invention of the Cotton Gin

Positive Consequences	Negative Consequences

The Alien and Sedition Acts

Matthew Lyon was an angry man in 1798, but that was nothing new to him. As a Republican in the Federalist stronghold of Vermont, he was often in the minority, and in those days, tempers ran hot when it came to politics. As a member of the House, he got into a heated argument with Representative Robert Griswold of Connecticut, and the two men tumbled to the floor in a brawl, wielding a cane and fire tongs. His low opinion of John Adams was also well known; he had expressed it often enough in his newspaper. When the Sedition Act was passed, Lyon would either have to be quiet or face time in prison.

Effects of the Jay Treaty

Angry over the Jay Treaty, which the Federalists had passed in 1795, the French stubbornly refused to approve the ambassador sent by the incoming president, John Adams. Rather than give in to the demands of some hot-headed Federalists for war, Adams sent three men to France to try and work things out.

XYZ Affair

The American representatives were visited one night by three representatives of French Foreign Minister Talleyrand. If the Americans gave Talleyrand a bribe, they would be allowed to talk with him. The Americans refused to pay the bribe and returned home. Adams sent a report of this insult to Congress and referred to the French agents as X, Y, and Z, and so the incident was called the XYZ Affair.

The Alien and Sedition Acts

Federalists saw this as an opportunity for political advantage over the pro-French Republicans. With patriotism running high, they increased the size of the army and navy and began to capture armed French merchant ships at sea. They then went even further and passed the Alien and Sedition Acts in 1798. The Alien Act extended the time before a person could become a citizen from five years to 14 years. The reason behind this was that immigrants were all joining the Republican party. The law also gave the president power to deport undesirable aliens.

The Sedition Act was passed as a response to recent actions by the French. The Sedition Act made it a crime to spread "false, scandalous, and malicious" writing against the government, the president, or Congress that would bring any of them into contempt or disrepute. Under this law, 15 people were charged and ten found guilty. One of these was Matthew Lyon, who criticized "aristocratic hirelings from the English porcupine." The judge, who was an ardent Federalist, sentenced Lyon to four months in jail and a $1,000 fine. He was taken to a jail usually used for common criminals. Friends wanted to rescue him, but he told them to vote their opinion, and he was reelected by a very large margin. After friends paid the fine, he was released and then returned to Philadelphia accompanied by a long line of supporters. Rather than silencing criticism, the Sedition Act had only made the Federalists look like enemies of freedom.

A number of other critics were heard as well. The Virginia and Kentucky legislatures passed resolutions protesting the law. The secret authors of those resolutions were James Madison and Thomas Jefferson. The Alien Act was repealed, and the Sedition Act expired. The French saw that their policy had been a big mistake, and they accepted new American diplomats with proper dignity, without asking for a bribe. However, Matthew Lyon continued to speak his mind.

Name: ______________________ Date: ______________________

The Alien and Sedition Acts: Activity

Directions: Complete the graphic organizer for the vocabulary words listed below. Write a definition for each word and use it in a sentence. Use an online or print dictionary if you need help.

alien	Definition
	Sentence

sedition	Definition
	Sentence

Federalist	Definition
	Sentence

resolution	Definition
	Sentence

The Louisiana Purchase

Never had an opportunity like this come to the United States; Jefferson knew it, but he was still troubled by it. Here was a chance to buy 827,000 square miles of real estate, rid the nation of a dangerous neighbor, and allow room for expansion to the crest of the Rocky Mountains. It had come about in this way: France had lost its domain known as Louisiana to Spain in 1763, and French pride had been hurt in the process. In 1800, Napoleon had put pressure on Spain to return it, and the two nations had made a secret treaty whereby France could take it back whenever they chose. American diplomats heard rumors of this deal in 1801.

People didn't know much about the Louisiana Territory at the time. There were only a few settlements like St. Louis on its eastern fringe, but what it held in rivers, minerals, animals, and agricultural potential was anyone's guess. It was known there were many Native Americans there, but their numbers and friendliness were yet to be discovered. What was known was, in the hands of Spain, Louisiana was no threat to western development. If France moved back in, it could block American expansion and, at worst, become a hazard to the United States. Jefferson told American diplomats to use whatever means they could to prevent the transfer of the land from Spain to France.

Napoleon Sells the Louisiana Territory

That need was emphasized when the Spanish governor at New Orleans issued an order that would prevent Americans from depositing their goods at New Orleans while waiting for ships to transport them to world markets. Frontiersmen suspected the French were behind this and were willing to take steps to seize New Orleans. To calm them down, Jefferson sent James Monroe to Paris with instructions to buy New Orleans and Florida if France owned them. Before Monroe arrived, Napoleon had already decided to sell the Louisiana Territory. He had hoped to use the money to feed the people of Haiti while they produced sugar and tropical fruit for France, but his plan had fallen through. Led by Toussaint L'Ouverture, the Haitians had destroyed a French army sent to control them. Without Haiti, Napoleon did not need the Louisiana Territory.

Senate Approves Purchase

The price agreed upon for the Louisiana Territory was $15,000,000, one-fourth of which was to pay damage claims by Americans against the French; however, the deal bothered the president's conscience. No specific authority had been given by the Constitution to buy land, and he had always opposed stretching the language of the Constitution. He thought about seeking a Constitutional amendment, but Monroe advised him that Napoleon would back out if they delayed. The temptation was too strong, and Jefferson took the offer to Congress. On October 20, 1803, the senate approved the purchase of the Louisiana Territory. The territory now belonged to the United States.

What Were the Results?

It would take many years before the full potential of the Louisiana Territory would be known. Lewis and Clark's expedition was a helpful beginning in discovering the Upper Missouri River region, and Zebulon Pike was sent to find the source of the Arkansas River. Other secrets of the region would be discovered by fur trappers and pioneers.

Name: ______________________ Date: ______________

The Louisiana Purchase: Activity

Directions: Use the information from the reading selection to complete the chart.

Central Idea	
Supporting Detail 1	**Supporting Detail 2**
Supporting Detail 3	**Supporting Detail 4**
Summary	

Marbury v. Madison

John Marshall

In 1801, President Adams appointed John Marshall to the Supreme Court. It wasn't easy finding high-quality men for the Court in those days. The job required long horseback rides, staying in dingy inns, and listening to endless debates between lawyers. The Court only met briefly each year in the capital because so few cases were appealed. The workload was so light that Chief Justice Jay took time to negotiate a treaty in England. His successor, Oliver Ellsworth, was also sent on a diplomatic mission to France.

John Marshall had been a captain during the Revolution and then became a lawyer. He was a delegate to Virginia's convention ratifying the Constitution and served a term in the U.S. House. He was a quiet, friendly man. He did not appear impressive, but in debate or a courtroom, he moved quickly to the heart of issues. As a strong Federalist, he had won the admiration of Washington and Adams. Since he was only 46 years old, he could take the punishment of the travels required by the job.

Judiciary Act of 1789

The Supreme Court consisted of one chief justice and five associate justices at that time. The issues they could decide were set in Article III of the Constitution and can be summarized as: (1) appellate power in cases involving federal law and treaties and (2) direct power in disputes between states and cases involving ambassadors. When not meeting as a court, the justices "rode circuit" to hear cases. The Judiciary Act of 1789 said that a circuit court (court of appeals) would consist of two Supreme Court justices and a district judge. Traveling was the reason many qualified men were not interested in serving as judges.

"Midnight Judges"

In 1801, before he left office, Adams was appointing judges to fill newly created positions. Because they were appointed at the last minute, they were called "midnight judges." One of those was William Marbury, who was appointed to be a justice of the peace in the District of Columbia. After confirmation by the Senate, their commission papers were signed by the president and then taken to the office of the secretary of state. Once the Great Seal of the United States was on these documents, the commission would be issued, and the new judges could perform their duties.

Marbury v. Madison

Thomas Jefferson succeeded Adams as president. Jefferson's choice for secretary of state was James Madison. When Madison saw the judicial commissions on his desk, he asked Jefferson what to do with them. Jefferson realized that he could keep 16 Federalists, appointed by Adams, from holding office simply by not issuing their commissions. Jefferson told Madison to hold them. Marbury sued in the Supreme Court for his commission. In 1803, the Supreme Court, led by Chief Justice John Marshall, decided the landmark case known as *Marbury v. Madison.* Under the Judiciary Act, Marbury was entitled to his commission. However, the Constitution had not given the Supreme Court authority to hear this type of case as original jurisdiction. No government official could go beyond the powers given by the Constitution, including the Supreme Court, so the Judiciary Act of 1789 was declared unconstitutional.

What Were the Results?

For the first time, the Court established the principle of judicial review and its power to declare an act of Congress invalid.

Name: ______________________________ Date: ____________________

Marbury v. Madison: Activity

Directions: Complete the graphic organizer by providing the impact of each event. Support your answer with details from the reading selection.

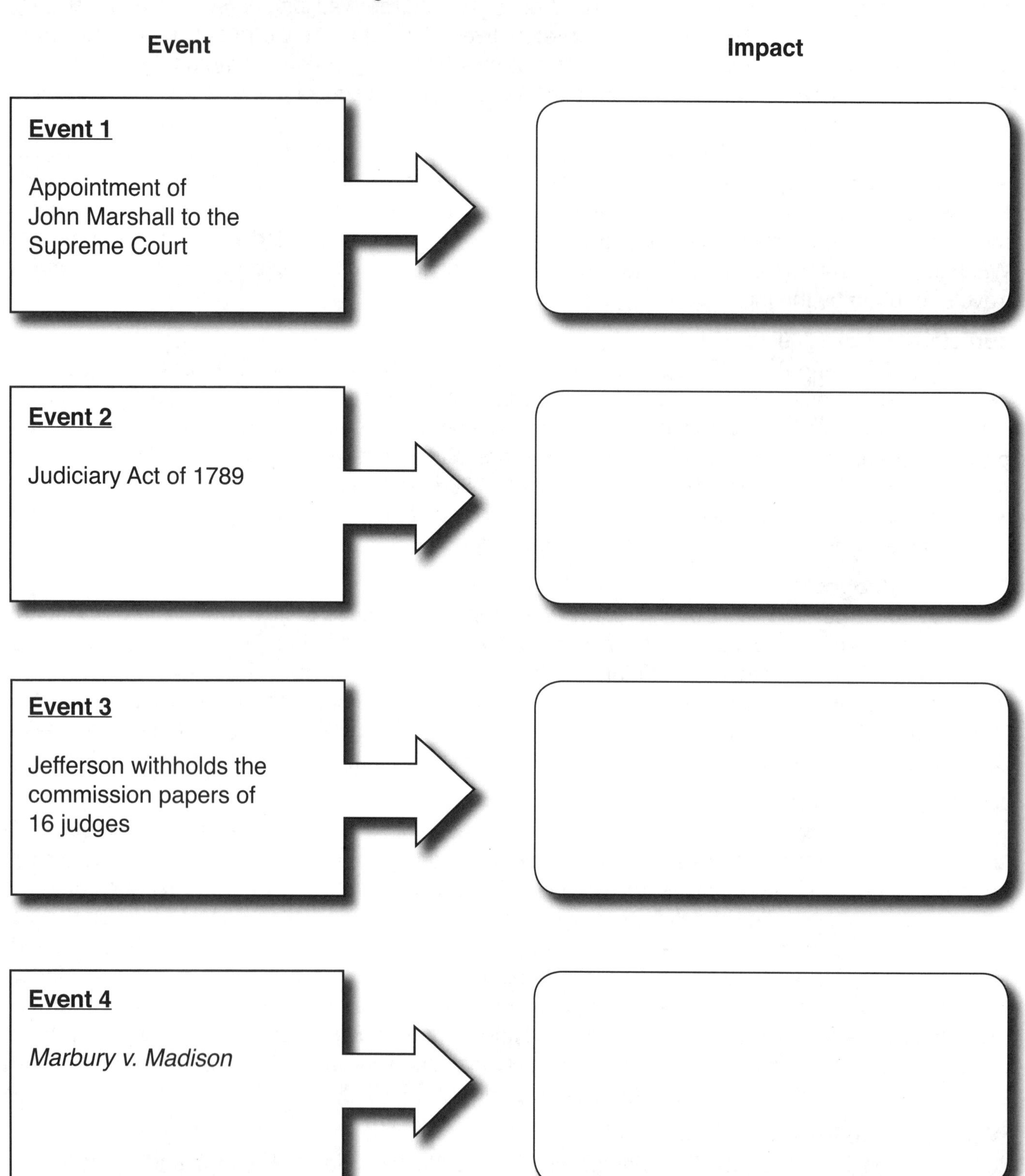

Robert Fulton and the Steamboat

Robert Fulton

Water transportation was little different in 1800 than it had been 1,800 years before. It was still boats powered by wind or oars, moving a little faster than the current downstream and painfully slow upstream. On America's western rivers, a variety of canoes, rafts, and flatboats could be seen. But one American had a vision of an improved method, and while critics called it "folly," Robert Fulton proved not only that steam could drive boats, but that steamboats could bring great profit to their owners and lower prices to consumers.

Robert Fulton

Fulton was creative from his youth. When he was ten, he made his own pencils; when he was 13, he invented a skyrocket; and at 14, he devised a manually powered paddlewheel for his fishing boat. When he was 17, he began working for a silversmith. After a serious illness, he began to paint miniatures and traveled to England in 1787 to visit his famous artist uncle, Benjamin West. While there, his interest turned from art to engineering.

Fulton in Europe

In 1794, he worked on a system of lifting boats over difficult spots in canals and invented a dredging machine for cutting canal channels. In 1797, he left England and went to France where he studied languages, mathematics, chemistry, and physics. He offered to build a submarine for the French government. On the first test, his submarine dove 25 feet and stayed under seven minutes; the second test lasted 17 minutes. When Napoleon showed little interest in his device, Fulton was lured back to England. The English were more interested in his invention of an underwater mine called a coffer than in submarines. A mine was used against a French ship, and an angry public protested that it was an unfair weapon. After receiving payment from the English, he returned to the United States in 1806 and began working on the device that would be his crowning achievement: the steamboat.

The Steamboat

He was not the only one trying to build a steam-powered boat. His brother-in-law, John Stevens, tried out the *Little Juliana* in 1806 but was not satisfied with the results. Fulton completed his *Clermont* the next year. His project was done so quietly that newspapers paid little attention to it, but when it chugged up the Hudson River from New York in August 1807, a fair-sized crowd came out to watch and to scoff at what was called "Fulton's Folly." To the surprise of scoffers, the *Clermont* arrived in Albany 32 hours later. In 1811, his *New Orleans* was the first steamboat to travel down the Ohio and Mississippi Rivers. During the War of 1812, he designed a steam warship named *Fulton the First*, but it did not see action because the war ended.

By the 1830s, many steamboats moved up and down rivers, bringing down the costs of shipping and traveling for the American public. Steamboat accidents were common, as unsafe boilers, snags in river bottoms, and sandbars took their toll. However, it was the beginning of exciting changes in transportation.

Name: ______________________________ Date: ____________________

Robert Fulton and the Steamboat: Activity

Directions: Use information from the reading selection to answer the questions.

1. What did Fulton invent during his youth?	2. What did Fulton do to improve the canal system in England?
3. What military devices did Fulton build or create?	4. What achievement did Fulton have with steam-powered boats?

Events Leading Up to the War of 1812

Impressment of Sailors

In 1803, war broke out between England and France. The leader of France was Napoleon. His goal was not just to defeat an army, but to conquer the nation.

At first, Americans were able to take advantage of the situation. American ships that weren't permitted to carry goods between the French West Indies and France before the war were now allowed. The English considered that illegal and captured American ships. That was bad enough, Americans thought, but even worse was the impressment of sailors. The English began to stop American ships and search them for deserters from the Royal Navy. If they found a sailor who looked strong, they often took him anyway. It did no good for the sailor to complain; if he did, he would be flogged with a cat-o'-nine-tails. He would wait, and at the first opportunity, he would escape.

Tecumseh

The *Chesapeake-Leopard* Affair

In 1807, the U.S. Navy ship *Chesapeake* was stopped by the British Navy ship the *Leopard*. The captain of the *Leopard* demanded that the captain of the *Chesapeake* allow his officers to search for deserters. When the American commander refused, the *Leopard* opened fire. The *Chesapeake* was not prepared for battle, and after being hit many times, it surrendered. The British sailed off with four members of the crew. Americans were outraged, but because the United States had little army or navy, all Jefferson could do was order English ships to leave American ports.

Battle of Tippecanoe

There were other problems between the United States and England. People on the frontier worried about Tecumseh, a Shawnee chief. Tecumseh disputed the surrender of tribal land under the Treaty of Greenville. Tecumseh and some members of his tribe left the Ohio area around 1808 and went to the Indiana territory to join up with his brother, Tenskwatawa. His brother, a religious leader known as the Prophet, lived close to where the Tippecanoe and Wabash rivers joined. Tecumseh began recruiting tribes to join a confederation.

In 1811, Governor William Henry Harrison formed an army and attacked the Prophet's camp at Tippecanoe while Tecumseh was away recruiting. The Native Americans withdrew after the battle and left behind guns with English markings on them. To American Westerners, this was proof that the Native Americans were being armed by the British.

What Were the Results?

Henry Clay of Kentucky became the Speaker of the House in 1811, and he and his friends took a hard line toward England. They received the nickname War Hawks. The term was intended as an insult, but they liked it and used it as a badge of pride. Angered by English restrictions on trade, the impressment of sailors, and Western fears, Congress moved toward war in 1812.

Name: ______________________ Date: ______________________

Events Leading Up to the War of 1812: Activity

Directions: Explain why each event angered Americans and moved the nation closer toward war with England.

1. Impressment of Sailors

2. *Chesapeake-Leopard* Affair

3. Battle of Tippecanoe

The Missouri Compromise of 1820

Henry Clay

The War of 1812 brought the nation together, and people were just beginning to think of themselves as Americans. For a time, there was only one political party. By 1820, however, the mood was changing. America had grown from 13 states in 1790 to 22 states and from a population of under 4 million to 9.6 million. The area east of the Mississippi River was growing rapidly; in some states, the population doubled every ten years. The region west of the mighty river was also beginning to fill in as well. Missouri, with 19,000 people in 1810, had 66,000 in 1820. Missouri Territory applied for statehood in 1817, but no action was taken for two years. In 1819, Maine also wanted statehood, which kept a balance of slave and free states. When Congress passed an enabling act, state governments were to be formed by Maine and Missouri.

An Amendment is Proposed

Then something simple became complicated. Representative James Tallmadge of New York wanted an amendment to the enabling legislation. He proposed that no more slaves be taken to Missouri, and those born of slave parents in the state would be freed at the age of 25. Two issues were raised by that proposal. Did Congress have any right to tell Missouri that it had to accept statehood with strings attached? More important at the time was this new limitation on the future of slavery.

At the same time Missouri was being discussed, the Senate was debating the new Adams-Onis Treaty with Spain. By it, the United States acquired Florida but gave up any claim to Texas. Large areas might be opened to settlement in the northern regions of Louisiana, but no further growth would be possible for the South. Now Tallmadge was going to end slavery in Missouri sometime in the next 30 or 40 years. Many in the southern states had seen the faults of slavery but had labeled it a "necessary evil." Without slaves, they could not produce cotton, tobacco, or rice as cheaply as they could with slave labor. People in the southern states had never thought of themselves as a unit before, pulling together against outsiders. For the first time, the South rallied around slavery; instead of admitting that it was wrong, they defended it as a "positive good."

Think About It

People of the South saw northerners as oppressors wanting to take away their rights. In the same way, people from western states saw themselves as different from easterners. The nation was moving toward deep divisions that would lead to a civil war 40 years later.

A Compromise is Offered

A compromise was offered by Senator Jesse Thomas of Illinois. By it, Missouri would enter the Union as a slave state, Maine as a free state, and the territories in the Louisiana Purchase north of 36°30' would be free. It barely passed. Then Missouri confused things again by writing a constitution that would prohibit free African Americans from entering the state. Another hot debate took place in Congress, but Henry Clay worked out a deal. A resolution was passed saying that Missouri must never use its power to take away the rights of any American citizen. Missouri promised to abide by the rule, and it was admitted as a state in August 1821.

Name: ______________________________ Date: ____________________

The Missouri Compromise of 1820: Activity

Directions: Summarize the involvement of each person in Missouri and Maine achieving statehood.

James Tallmadge	Jesse Thomas	Henry Clay
Summary:	**Summary:**	**Summary:**

The Election of 1824

The writers of the Constitution had done an amazing job, but they could not predict everything that might happen in the future. An example of this occurred in the presidential election of 1800. Political parties had developed by then, and Thomas Jefferson and Aaron Burr tied in the electoral vote with 73 votes each. The Constitution gave the House of Representatives the job of picking a winner, and it chose Jefferson. To keep it from happening again, the Twelfth Amendment was passed. It said that the president and vice president were to be chosen by separate ballots. If no one had a majority of votes, the House would choose the president from among the top three candidates, and the Senate would choose the vice president from the top two. No one at the time could have guessed how soon the Twelfth Amendment would be used to select a president.

1824 Election

In 1824, everyone knew that President James Monroe's second term was coming to an end, and there was only one political party. The Federalist Party was dying out, and only a few were still active in politics. There were no political conventions or presidential primaries at that time. Instead, candidates were chosen by a caucus of party leaders in Congress who picked their choice for president. The caucus in 1824 chose William Crawford, the Secretary of the Treasury. However, most party leaders did not attend the caucus—they had their own candidates to run. Among these were Secretary of State John Quincy Adams, Speaker of the House Henry Clay, Secretary of War John C. Calhoun, and General Andrew Jackson. Each was from a different state, and only Adams was from the New England region.

Until this time, electors had all been chosen by the state legislatures, but a few states now allowed the voters to make the choice. They did choose the most popular candidate: Jackson (153,000), followed by Adams (108,000), Clay (47,000), and Crawford (46,000). No candidate had the majority of electoral votes; the order of votes received was Jackson, Adams, Crawford, and Clay. Since Clay was fourth, he was out of the running. But as Speaker of the House, he had great influence.

Adams and Jackson Compete for the Presidency

By this time, Crawford was not a possible choice. He had suffered a stroke, and while he was on his way to recovery, his health problems could not be ignored. Both Jackson and Adams believed they should be chosen. Adams was well educated and had been a diplomat and an outstanding secretary of state. Jackson was a military hero who had served as a judge and briefly as a senator.

Adams Becomes President

Clay went to Adams' house one night, and the two men talked for hours. Clay secretly decided that Adams was best for the job and applied pressure on members wavering between the two men. With Clay's help, Adams won the election, even though he was second in popular and in electoral votes. Jackson was angry and felt that he deserved the job. When Adams picked Clay to be secretary of state, Jackson and his followers were sure a corrupt deal had been struck between Adams and Clay. The result was Adams was able to do little as president because Jackson supporters in Congress blocked him.

Name: ______________________________ Date: ____________________

The Election of 1824: Activity

Directions: Think about what you have read and then answer the questions below. Cite evidence from the reading selection to support your answers.

1. What effect did the Twelfth Amendment have on the presidential election of 1824?

2. What influence did Henry Clay have on the selection of John Q. Adams as president?

Improvements in Transportation

The coming of the steamboat was only the beginning of a great change that occurred in America. Prior to 1800, Americans were plagued by slow transportation. Roads were often paths cut through the forest with stumps just low enough that a wagon could pass over them. Rivers were the main method of getting goods to market, but they could run low, flood, or have a current too swift at points for safe passage. The need for improvement to travel was obvious, and different approaches were used to accomplish it.

Roads

Construction began on the National Road in 1811; it was to be a turnpike built between Cumberland, Maryland, and Wheeling, Virginia. It was America's first superhighway, and it was completed in 1818. It was 30 feet wide in the mountains and 66 feet wide elsewhere. With solid bridges and a gravel base, it seemed like a work of wonder to travelers. By the 1830s, a trip from Washington to Wheeling took only thirty hours! Other privately owned turnpikes were built as well, but most roads continued to be very poor.

Canals

Another improvement was the Erie Canal. Built between Albany and Buffalo, New York, from 1817 to 1825, it was an enormous success. It was 364 miles long, four feet deep, and 40 feet wide. It carried the commerce of the Great Lakes to New York and made it the center of the nation's trade. For shippers, the cost dropped from 20 cents a ton mile to 2 cents. Other states also built canals, especially Ohio and Indiana, but theirs were never as successful as New York's. It did not take long for the canal era to end, however, as stiff new competition came from the railroad.

Railroads

In the early 1820s, English inventors began to work on steam engines to do work, and Americans who were aware of this saw the potential of railroads for America. In 1828, construction began on the Baltimore & Ohio (B&O) Railroad, and in 1830, thirteen miles of it opened for business. Soon other railroads were being built in America.

Traveling by train was regarded as an almost foolhardy thing for a person to do. Sparks from the locomotive's boiler blew back on passengers, and since many boilers were poorly made, explosions occurred. Railroads put on barrier cars that were piled high with cotton between the locomotive and the train to protect the customers.

Improvements came very quickly. The "Tom Thumb," the first American-built locomotive on the B&O, had a top speed of 15 mph but averaged only 5.5 mph. In a race with a horse, it lost because of mechanical failures, but it proved itself in the long pull by hauling 42 passengers with its 1.43 horsepower. In 1832, just two years after the "Tom Thumb" was built, the Mohawk and Hudson Railroad built the "Brother Jonathan," which was much heavier and more powerful. It could move at a top speed of 80 mph.

Americans quickly saw the importance of railroads, which could transport people far more rapidly than a stagecoach. Most railroads were constructed east-west, and this caused less contact between Northerners and Southerners. The North's railroads were far superior to those in the South, which would become a factor during the Civil War.

Name: ______________________ Date: ______________________

Improvements in Transportation Activity

Directions: Use information from the reading selection to complete the graphic organizer.

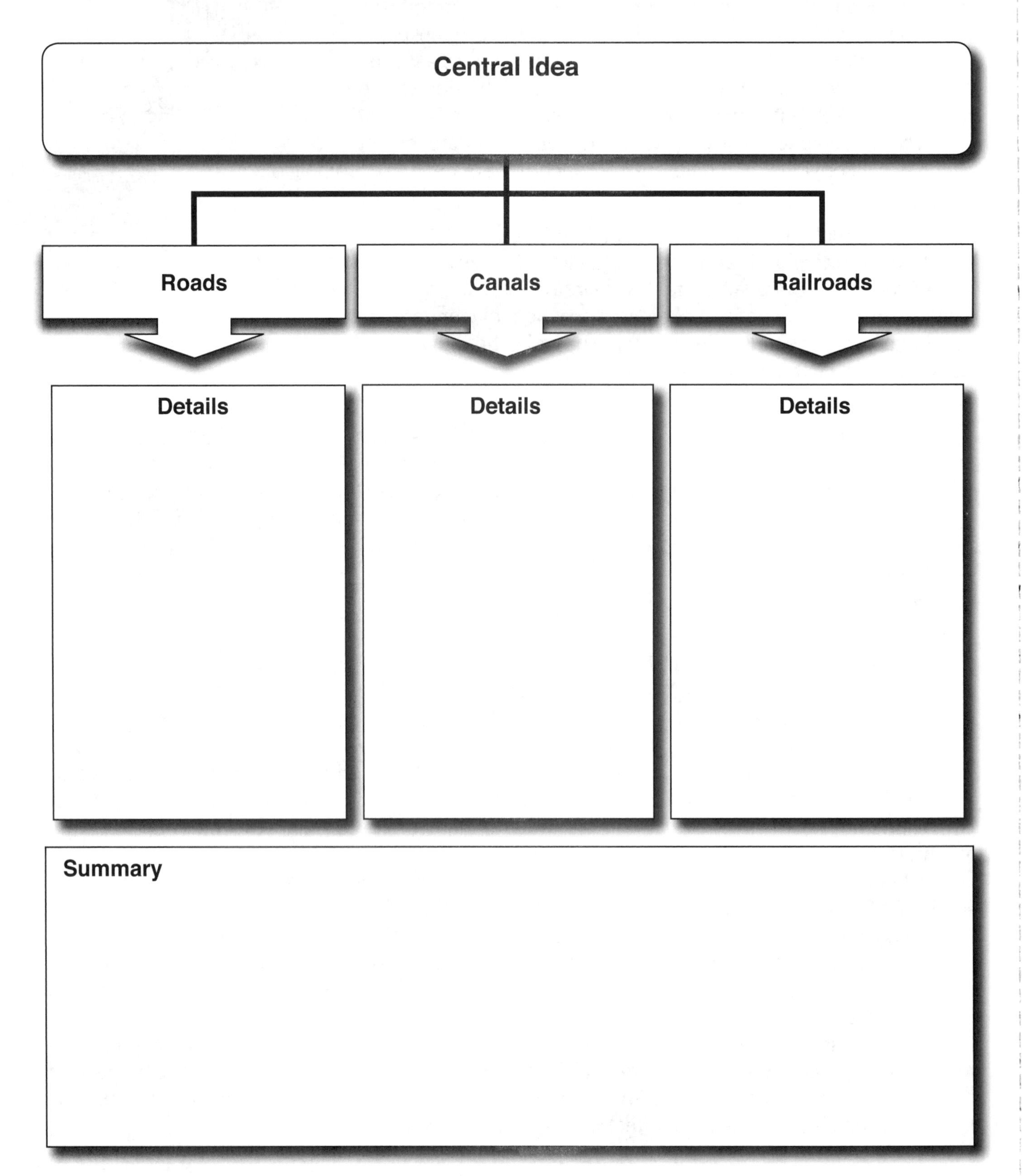

The Five "Civilized" Tribes Are Moved West

Native Americans in the United States were coming under increasing pressure in the 1820s. The small northern tribes were forced to leave valuable lands and were relocated to lands considered worthless. Meaningless treaties were signed by chiefs, and all tribal members were expelled. The southern tribes were larger and more organized, however. They were known as the Five "Civilized" Tribes because they had adopted many of the white settlers' customs: religion, houses, clothing, and even slaveholding. They included Cherokees, Creeks, Chickasaws, Choctaws, and Seminoles. The largest was the Cherokee nation. A Cherokee named Sequoyah was so impressed with the "talking leaves" (written words) of the settlers that he developed a written alphabet using the 85 syllables in his language.

Creation of Arkansas Territory and Indian Territory

White settlers wanted the Native Americans' valuable cotton lands for themselves. President James Monroe felt Native Americans should exchange their lands for lands west of the Mississippi River. In 1824, he approved the first plan for native removal. On January 27, 1825, in a special message to the Senate, he requested the creation of the Arkansas Territory and Indian Territory. President John Quincy Adams was pressured by Georgia's governor and politicians to remove the Cherokee and Creek nations. In 1825, Chief William McIntosh, a Creek leader, signed a treaty giving up tribal lands to the state of Georgia. The treaty was very unpopular with most tribal members. In April 1825, Chief Menewa and his soldiers killed McIntosh for signing the treaty. In 1826, Chief Menewa, a member of the Creek National Council delegation, went to Washington, D.C., to protest the treaty. President Adams negotiated a new clause that would cede less tribal lands to Georgia. Governor George Troup of Georgia was furious with this decision and began pressuring the Native Americans to leave, regardless of what President Adams thought. In 1836, Chief Menewa would join the long line of Creeks heading for Indian Territory.

Indian Removal Act

In 1829, gold prospectors flooded into the Cherokee lands in northern Georgia. The Cherokee tried to remove the settlers from their lands. In 1830, President Jackson signed the Indian Removal Act. This law forced the Cherokee and other nations to leave their lands and relocate to an area known as the Indian Territory. This new homeland is now known as eastern Oklahoma. Choctaw removal in 1831 was slowed by ice on the Mississippi River and heavy snows in the Arkansas swamps through which they passed. Desperately short on food, many starved while the man who was supposed to supply them stayed at home in Nashville because it was too cold to travel. The devasting journey became known as the "Trail of Tears."

Cherokee and Seminoles Fight Removal

The Cherokees fought removal in the courts, and the Supreme Court agreed that their treaty rights had been violated, but Jackson refused to support the verdict of the Court. He was said to have remarked, "John Marshall has made his decision; now let him enforce it." In 1836, Cherokees began relocating to the Indian Territory. The remaining Cherokees were forced to leave in 1838, but some escaped to the mountains of North Carolina, where their descendants still live. The rest walked the "Trail of Tears," and many of them died on their way to Indian Territory.

Seminoles hid in Florida's swamps. Led by Chief Osceola, they stubbornly refused to move out. Assisted by runaway slaves, the Seminoles were at war with the U.S. government. Osceola was captured in October 1837 and died on January 30, 1838. After his death, most of his followers surrendered and relocated west. A few stayed behind in Florida.

Name: ______________________ Date: ______________

The Five "Civilized" Tribes Are Moved West: Activity

Directions: Use the information in the reading selection to develop a time line (from earliest to latest event) showing the history of Native American removal from tribal lands. The first one is done for you.

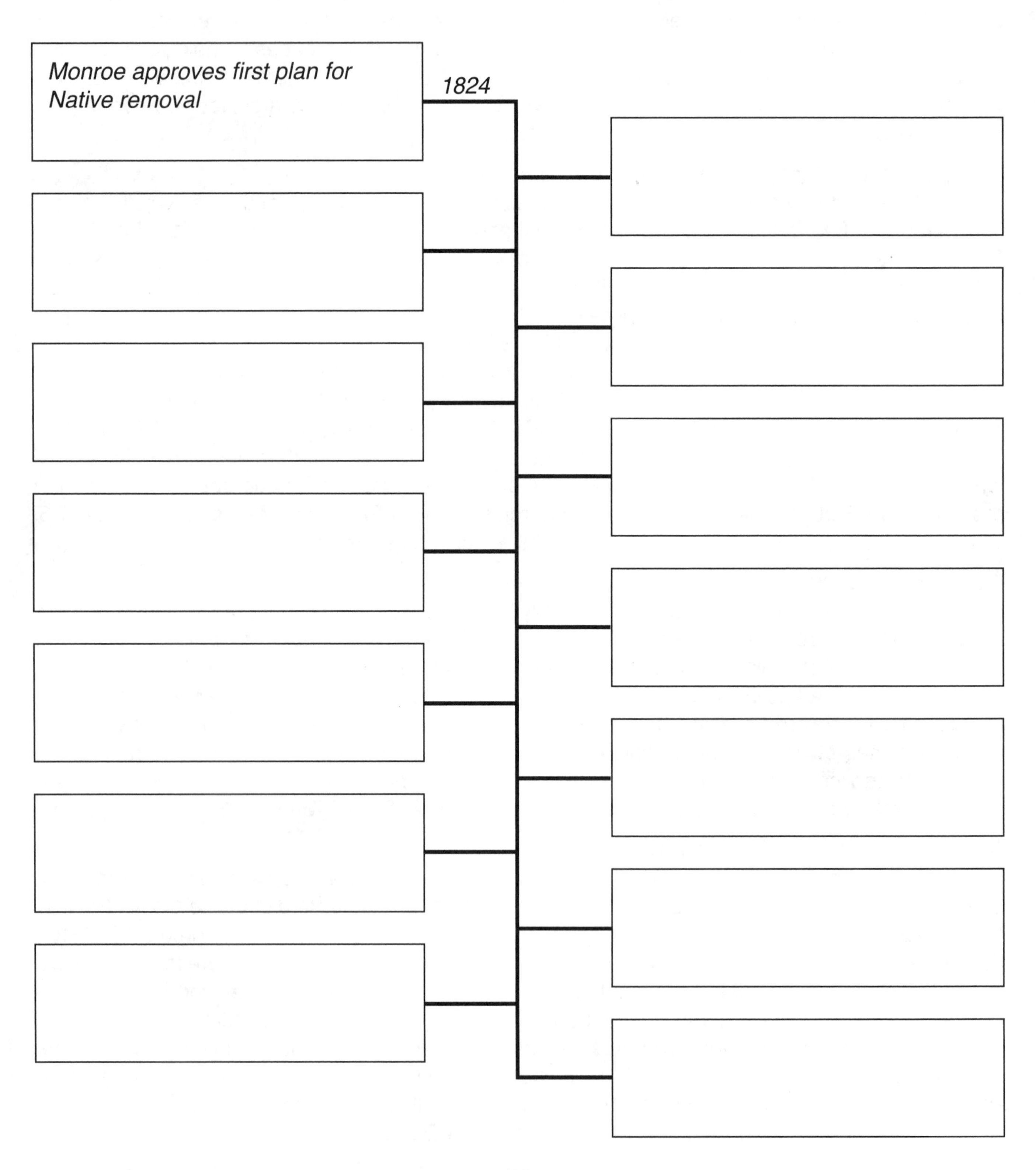

Jackson Opposes the Central Banking System

State Versus Federal Rights

President Jackson was a man with strong opinions on many issues, and rather than argue forever about what should be done, he acted. He had reacted strongly when Vice President John C. Calhoun of South Carolina said states had a right to cancel any law passed by Congress if it was unconstitutional (nullification). This would make the states more important than the federal government, and they could decide whether or not to obey a law. At the Jefferson birthday dinner in 1830, President Jackson looked across the table at Calhoun and offered a toast: "To the federal Union, it must be preserved." In 1833, South Carolina said it would nullify the tariff passed in 1832. Jackson warned that he would send an army against the state, and few doubted he would do it. South Carolina backed down.

Andrew Jackson

Creating a Central Banking System

If Jackson disagreed with Calhoun, he was even more angry with Nicholas Biddle, president of the Second Bank of the United States. Government banks were nothing new. England, France, and most European countries had a central bank. The United States government had created the First Bank of the United States in 1791 as its central bank. It was never popular with Republicans. The bank's charter expired in 1811, and Congress had not renewed it.

By 1816, that was seen as a mistake, and a new central bank, the Second Bank of the United States, was chartered for 20 years. There were good reasons to have the bank. It made it easy for the government to borrow money and gave it a safe place to deposit money. It also kept an eye on state banks and kept them from lending more money than they should.

There were also problems with the Bank, however. There was too much power in the hands of Biddle. He was the only member of its board who understood what the Bank was doing. It also lent money to leading political leaders and did not worry about how quickly they paid it back. The Bank bought ads in newspapers, and the owners of the newspapers knew that they were required to write articles friendly to the Bank, or they would lose the advertising.

State banks did not like the Second Bank and thought it interfered with their ability to loan money to risky customers. President Jackson didn't like banks, which could mean trouble when the Bank asked for a new charter.

Election of 1832

Many political leaders in 1832 considered Jackson high-handed and wanted Henry Clay to run as the National Republican candidate. Clay and Daniel Webster persuaded Biddle to ask for his bank charter in 1832, rather than wait four years. That way, the Bank would become the main issue in the campaign. A bill to recharter the Bank passed in Congress, but Jackson vetoed it, saying the Bank let the rich use the government for selfish purposes. Jackson easily won the election and began to kill the Bank immediately. He withdrew government funds when he paid its bills. When money came in from taxes, it was withdrawn and placed in state banks. When its charter expired, the Second Bank was chartered as a Pennsylvania bank, but it did not last long and closed permanently in 1841.

Name: ______________________________ Date: ______________________

Jackson Opposes the Central Banking System: Activity

Directions: Use information from the reading selection to complete each activity.

Activity One: List the pros and cons of having a central bank.

Pros	Cons

Activity Two: What actions did President Jackson take to "kill" the Second Bank of the United States?

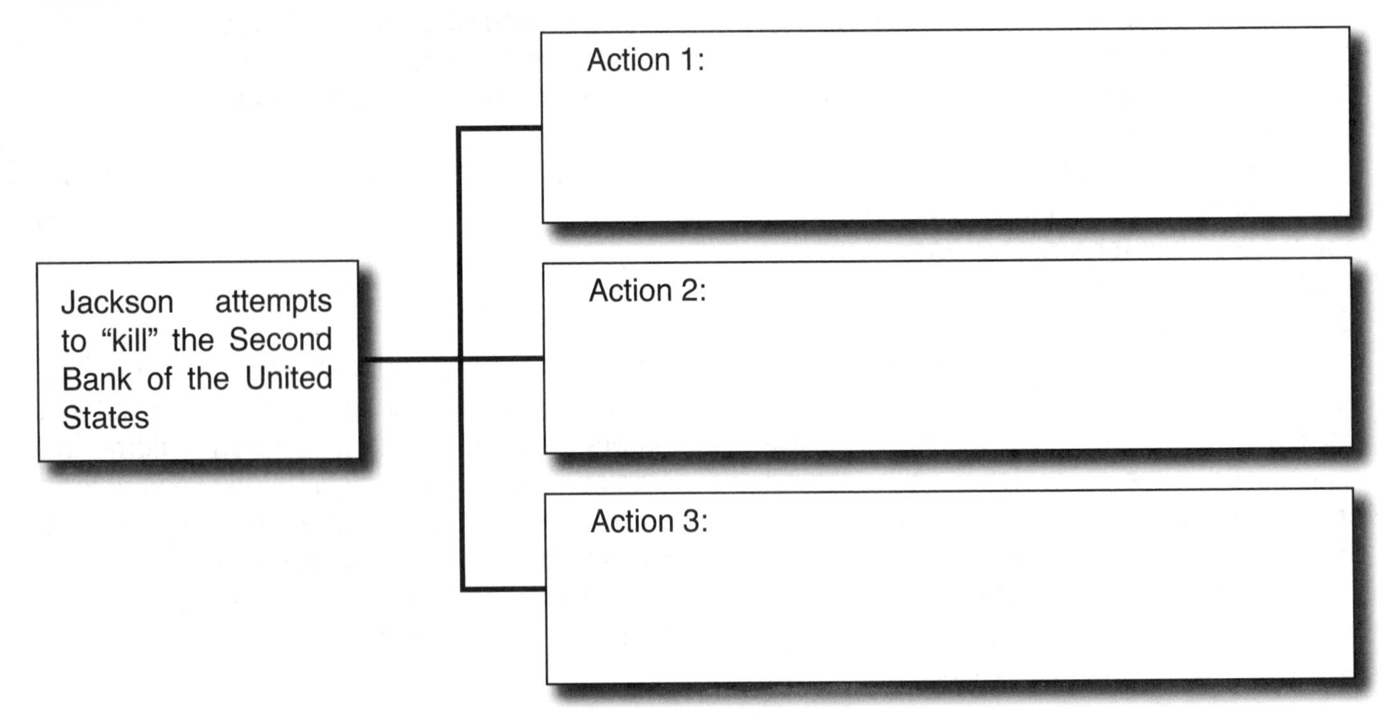

The North Develops an Industrial Economy

Thomas Jefferson had dreamed of an agricultural nation, with each man working for himself. That idea was still strong in the South in 1840 but was losing out in the Northeast. Factories developed, especially in New England where land was poor and fast-flowing streams produced water power capable of running machines. Textile mills were built, and that opened job opportunities. As transportation improved, anything produced in a Rhode Island factory could be sold anywhere in the United States or Europe.

Young lady working in a textile mill

Textile Industry

New inventions came along, increasing the need for factories. In 1810, there were only 77 patents issued, but in 1830, 544 were issued. New products meant more jobs and more factories. Companies were formed. Sometimes they had only one owner; others were corporations with stockholders. In small companies, the company president knew the employees; but as companies got larger, they became more impersonal.

Early Textile Mills and Factories

Early textile mills are a good example. New England towns worried that unless they created jobs, the young people would leave, so they built a mill to employ local workers. Girls were recruited from surrounding farms. They lived in supervised boardinghouses owned by the mills. For the girls, this was a way to earn money to help support their family. It also allowed them the freedom to leave home and live on their own for a time before they married.

Mills at first tried to make the setting as homey as possible. Flowers were put on window ledges, and little sayings from Ben Franklin or the Bible might be on the equipment for the girls to read and think about during the day. Lecturers were sometimes brought in to give speeches. A pleasant and moral atmosphere was what they wanted.

Each day, the girls would be awakened by a bell before sunrise, eat breakfast, march to the mill, and work about 12 hours for low wages. In the evening, the girls marched back to the boardinghouse, ate supper, and were in bed by 9 P.M. in a small room shared by up to five other girls. It did not take long for them to tire of this routine, and soon there were vacancies at the mill. Others worked there too. Child labor was common, with boys and girls eight years old and up working 10 to 12 hours a day. Sometimes whole families were hired. All of this meant little chance for children to attend school.

As the factory got larger, new workers were hired from England, Ireland, or Europe. Most of these young workers were girls who had little education, some of whom spoke no English. Factory owners were now less interested in caring for the workers and more interested in making money. They took away the flower boxes and the sayings. The mills were dirty and noisy. Mills were cold in the winter and hot in the summer. Many workers developed lung disease caused by inhaling the lint particles in the air.

Some workers tried to form unions, but they were not popular with the public at the time and were often declared illegal by the courts. Workers knew that newly arrived immigrants would gladly replace them on their jobs, so they were in a poor position to demand higher wages or shorter hours.

Name: ______________________ Date: ______________

The North Develops an Industrial Economy: Activity

Directions: In the graphic organizer record key details from the reading selection about the topic. Use the details to write a summary.

Topic: Life of a Textile Mill Worker

Early Textiles Mills

Key Details

Factory Textiles Mills

Key Details

Summary

Sam Houston Leads Texans to Independence

In the early 1830s, Texas was still part of Mexico, but its people were much different from those south of the Rio Grande. Texas had been a neglected part of Spanish territory until the Mexicans gained freedom. In 1820, Moses Austin had an idea of bringing American Catholic settlers into Texas, but he died before it could be arranged. His son, Stephen Austin, followed through with his idea, and in 1823 the terms were accepted. He was to settle 300 Catholic families in Texas. Each family would receive 177 acres for farming and 13,100 acres of grazing land. Austin would receive $1 for each eight acres of land, and when 200 families had come in, he got a bonus of 65,000 acres. Other colonies were established as well, but Austin's was the largest and most important.

Sam Houston

Sam Houston was one of the people who came to Texas. His family had moved from Virginia to Tennessee, but he did not like the farm work. So he left home and went to live with the Cherokee. During the War of 1812, he was in Jackson's army at the Battle of Horseshoe Bend and was badly wounded. After the war, he became a lawyer and was elected governor of Tennessee. When he and his wife broke up, he resigned as governor and went back to live with the Cherokee. In 1832, he went to Texas.

By 1835, relations between Texas and Mexico were very bad, which led to a revolution. The first battles were disasters for the Texans. On February 23, 1836, General Santa Anna surrounded the defenders of the Alamo, who fought until March 6th to the last man. At Goliad, the Texans were defeated again. The Texans turned to Sam Houston to be their leader; however, Houston's strategy bothered many. He retreated and burned fields so that Santa Anna's army would have to bring up all their supplies from Mexico. While he moved back, he trained his men so that when the time was right, they would be ready to win.

Battle of San Jacinto Creek

It was on April 21, 1836, at San Jacinto Creek that Houston decided to attack. His men charged Santa Anna's camp, shouting "Remember the Alamo," and "Remember Goliad." They won a quick victory. Prisoners were rounded up, but they could not find Santa Anna. Two days later, he was discovered in a corporal's uniform. Since he had been president of Mexico, Houston forced him to sign a statement giving Texas its independence. After Santa Anna was released, he said he had no authority to give Texas independence, and it was still part of Mexico; also, the boundary of Texas was in dispute. Mexico said Texas was the region north of the Nueces River, while Texans claimed the land south to the Rio Grande.

From Independence to Statehood

The next few years were hard on Texas. It wanted to be part of the United States, but many northern politicians did not want Texas because it allowed slavery. Texas was recognized as independent by England, France, and the United States, but it lived under the threat that Mexico would send an army against it. It was not until after James Polk was elected U.S. president in 1844 that progress was made. Because Polk supported expansion into Texas, the outgoing president, John Tyler, pushed through a joint resolution admitting Texas to the Union. Mexico was angry and did not accept this as the final word. The issue of Texas and the boundary would be settled by war.

Name: ______________________________ Date: ____________________

Sam Houston Leads Texans to Independence: Activity

Directions: Research the life of one of the people listed in the box below. Use your research to complete the graphic organizer.

Stephen Austin	Sam Houston	Jim Bowie	Davy Crockett
William Travis	James Fannin	Antonio López de Santa Anna	

His Life Before the Texas Revolution:
His Role in the Texas Revolution:
His Life After the Texas Revolution:

The Oregon Territory

The Fur Trade

Even before Lewis and Clark reached Oregon in 1805, there was an American presence there. Captain Robert Gray traveled to the Pacific Northwest coast in 1787 seeking sea otter furs to trade with China in exchange for silk, porcelain, and tea. In 1791, he returned to the area and explored the coast. On May 11, 1792, he discovered a river that he named after his ship, the *Columbia.* His discovery allowed the United States to lay claim to the Oregon territory.

There was a fortune to be made in Oregon. John Jacob Astor established a fort in Oregon in 1811 that he named Astoria. It was sold to the Northwest Company, a British firm, which merged with Hudson's Bay Company in 1821. Hudson's Bay sent Dr. John McLoughlin to Oregon to take over its land operations, but American ships still used the coast. In fact, so many of these were New England-owned that the Native Americans referred to all white men as "Bostons."

Interest in Annexation and Settlement

American interest in Oregon grew very slowly, almost one man at a time. Dr. John Floyd of Virginia was a member of Congress who wanted the United States to annex it. Most people laughed at him. They said Oregon was too far away and that the natural boundary for the United States was the Rocky Mountains. The government was not going to act; however, private individuals did.

Hall Kelley was a Massachusetts schoolteacher who became excited over Oregon after he read the *Journal of Lewis and Clark.* After years of talking about Oregon, he went to Mexico, then through California, and on to Oregon. The governor of California did not trust him and sent a letter to McLoughlin accusing Kelley of being a cattle thief. Kelley did little in Oregon, but when he returned, he talked about what a marvelous place it was. One of those listening was Nathaniel Wyeth, who made two trips there.

Quick Fact

The United States and England agreed in 1846 to set the dividing line between the United States and Canada at the 49th parallel.

Missionaries

Missionaries were interested in converting the Native Americans to Christianity. Jason and Daniel Lee went as Methodist missionaries; Samuel Parker, Dr. Marcus Whitman, and Henry Spalding were Presbyterian missionaries; and Father De Smet went as a Catholic missionary. The journey of Dr. Whitman and Reverend Spalding was especially important because they brought their wives with them. It had always been thought that an overland journey was too hard for a woman to make, but that theory was proven wrong.

Oregon Trail

Enthusiasm for Oregon grew rapidly in the early 1840s. Many Americans wanted to go there because of free land, a sense of adventure, and a desire to make Oregon part of the United States. In 1843, a large wagon train of 1,000 people headed west from Independence, Missouri. Those who brought herds of cattle and oxen traveled too slowly for those who took only necessities, so the group divided between the light column and cow column.

The trip was never easy, but there were some things a group could do to improve their chances of a successful journey: (1) have good leaders and listen to them; (2) have good teams of oxen, mules, or horses, and have a sturdy wagon; and (3) be sure to travel light. Many pioneers overloaded the wagons, and when the team got tired, they had to throw off unneeded items. Discarded dishes, tables, clothes, etc., littered the trail.

Name: ______________________ Date: ______________

The Oregon Territory: Activity

Directions: Use information from the reading selection to complete the graphic organizer.

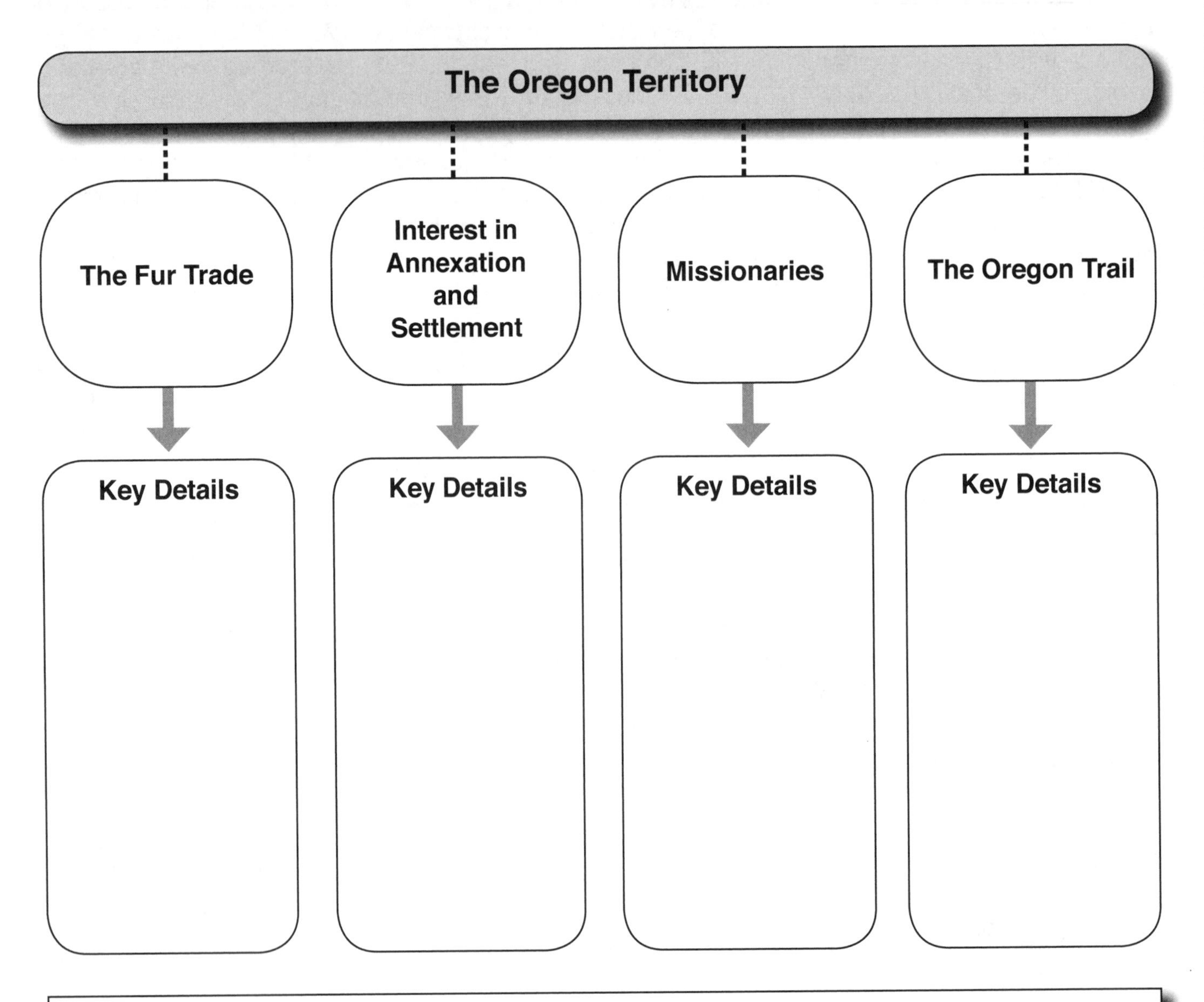

Summary

The Reform Movement in Pre-Civil War America

Calls for Reform

Many reformers were part of pre-Civil War America. The temperance movement called for limiting the use of or abstaining from alcohol. Horace Mann pushed for tax-supported public education; critics said it was too expensive. He won, and by 1860, all northern states had public schools. Some women and a few men favored equal rights for women, including the right to vote. National Women's Rights Conventions were held yearly to discuss these rights. Dorothea Dix brought about better treatment for the mentally ill. Dr. Elizabeth Blackwell, America's first woman physician, was an activist for public health. Some said society was beyond hope and formed utopian communities like Brook Farm in Massachusetts, New Harmony in Indiana, and Oneida in New York.

William Lloyd Garrison

Abolitionists

Of all reformers, none were as unpopular as abolitionists. Their goal was to end slavery, everywhere and immediately. Many admitted slavery was wrong, including some southerners, but abolitionists were more than against slavery—they wanted to destroy it and make slaveowners suffer for their terrible deeds against slaves. Many in the North did not share abolitionist views. They wanted southern products like cotton and tobacco and knew they would be hard to produce without slaves. They also felt that slavery was no harder than conditions in northern factories. They argued that southern states should be left alone to work out their own policies.

Quakers, a religious group, were the first critics of slavery. Samuel Cornish and John Russwurm, free African Americans, published the first African-American-owned newspaper, *Freedom's Journal,* in 1827. A Quaker named Benjamin Lundy published *The Genius of Universal Emancipation* at the same time. One of his assistants, William Lloyd Garrison, thought the Quaker approach was too slow and pushed for the immediate freeing of slaves. In 1831, he started *The Liberator,* warning, "I will be as harsh as truth and as uncompromising as justice." After stories spread that Nat Turner had been inspired to revolt because he had read the newspaper, Garrison got much more attention. Elijah Lovejoy, abolitionist editor of the *Alton Observer* in Illinois, advocated for the formation of an antislavery society in Illinois. He was murdered by a proslavery mob in November 1837 that was trying to destroy his press.

Gag Rule

In the 1830s, abolitionists began writing thousands of letters to Congress pushing it to act against slavery. Congress worried about these enough that the House passed the Gag Rule in 1836, which said that any protest against slavery would be tabled without discussion (in other words, totally ignored). When the postmaster general ordered that abolitionist material addressed to the South could be destroyed by postal officials, Congress did not criticize the ruling. Congress ignored abolitionist petitions, and the abolitionists used this as an example of how undemocratic methods by the South were used to silence criticism. No one was more vocal on the issue than John Quincy Adams. It was his belief that the rule restricted free speech. Rather than hurt the abolitionists, Congress' methods actually gained sympathy for them. In 1844, the Gag Rule was finally defeated.

Name: ______________________________ Date: ____________________

The Reform Movement in Pre-Civil War America: Activity

Directions: Use details in the reading selection to identify each individual, group, or movement.

Reformer, Group, or Movement	Identify
1. Temperance Movement	
2. Horace Mann	
3. Dorothea Dix	
4. Elizabeth Blackwell	
5. Brook Farm (Massachusetts)	
6. Quakers	
7. Samuel Cornish	
8. John Russwurm	
9. Benjamin Lundy	
10. William Lloyd Garrison	
11. Elijah Lovejoy	

Nicholas Trist and the Mexican-American War

As Nicholas Trist, chief clerk of the State Department, sat across from Mexican diplomats at Guadalupe-Hidalgo, he held the fate of California and New Mexico in his hands. He might have felt more important except he knew he was not supposed to be at that table on that day.

The United States and Mexico had been neighbors but not friends since Mexico had gained independence from Spain. Troubles began with arguments between officials and Santa Fe traders, the Texas Revolution, and disputes over Native American attacks and unpaid bills. Some Americans in California accepted Mexican rule without protest, but others wanted the United States to own it. In 1846, the Bear Flag Revolt broke out in California; when news reached the Americans involved, they flew the stars and stripes.

The Mexican-American War

Fighting had begun before war was declared. General Zachary Taylor had crossed the Nueces River, and one of his patrols was attacked. President Polk asked Congress for war, charging that "American blood has been shed on American soil." Most Americans supported the war at first, but Abraham Lincoln and John C. Calhoun both claimed the war was only a way to seize land.

During the Mexican War (1846–1848), American troops attacked on several fronts. Taylor's army advanced into the region south of the Rio Grande. General Stephen Kearny's army captured Santa Fe and moved across the deserts and mountains into California. General Winfield Scott led an invasion of Mexico, attacking Vera Cruz on the coast. Trist traveled with General Scott's army as an agent of the State Department. Trist was told that he could offer as much as $20 million for California and New Mexico and $5 million more for Lower California.

Trist's Relationship With Scott

Trist always tried to do his duty, but he found that traveling with Scott was very difficult. Scott did not like him because he thought Trist was a spy sent by the president to report any failure. After Trist became ill, Scott felt sorry for him and sent him a jar of jam. After that, a much better relationship existed between them. Trist was also finding it difficult to make peace with Mexico since its government was falling apart. In late 1847, Trist found a group willing to make peace.

Trist Defies President Polk

In November, Trist received orders to return home, but he did not know which way to go. If he returned, the war might go on endlessly. If he stayed, he defied a specific order from President Polk. He asked Scott what he should do, and Scott asked him to stay. He ignored the order and negotiated a peace treaty with Mexico.

Treaty of Guadalupe Hidalgo

The treaty was signed on February 2, 1848. In the treaty, Mexico gave up any claim to Texas and ceded Upper California and New Mexico to the United States in exchange for $15 million. The treaty also established the Texas boundary at the Rio Grande. President Polk was angry with Trist for defying orders, but he saw the need to end the war quickly, and the terms of the treaty were good. In March, the Senate ratified the Treaty of Guadalupe Hidalgo, and the war was officially over. The United States had gained 525,000 square miles of valuable land and new outlets for trade with Asia. President Polk got even with Trist for defying orders by firing him and refusing to pay his salary and accrued expenses. In 1871, Congress finally authorized reimbursing Trist for his salary and expenses.

Name: ______________________ Date: ______________________

Nicholas Trist and the Mexican-American War: Activity

Directions: Use the information from the reading selection to complete the chart.

Summarize in Your Own Words	
1. Nicholas Trist's Relationship With General Scott	
2. The Terms of the Treaty of Guadalupe Hidalgo	
3. Nicholas Trist's Relationship With President Polk	

The California Gold Rush

Early History of California

In the early history of California, settlements were scattered, with only a few missions, ranches, and towns in the territory. The climate and soil made life easy for settlers, and Native Americans provided a cheap source of labor. A few Americans went to California before 1840: fur trappers, whalers, and cattle buyers. Some arrived overland, but most came by sea around South America. Some settled; others, like Jedediah Smith, the mountain man, were just passing through.

Early American Settlers

Among the American settlers were Thomas Larkin, a leading merchant at Monterrey; John Marsh, who owned a big ranch; and Johann Sutter, who settled in northern California. Sutter was originally from Switzerland but had come to the United States in 1834 to avoid paying his debts. Five years later, he was in California, became a Mexican citizen, and borrowed money to buy land. When large numbers of Americans began coming overland to California, many stayed at Sutter's ranch while they rested after their long trip. He was a good host, but many took advantage of him.

Overland Trail

The overland trip was a difficult experience. The first settlers to try it, the Bidwell party, looked like scarecrows when they arrived in 1841. The next year, Lansford Hastings wrote a book, *The Emigrant's Guide to California,* giving suggestions on overland travel to would-be settlers. Not everything in the book had been checked out, and it included an unexplored shortcut that became known as the Hastings Cutoff. The Donner party tried the Hastings Cutoff in 1846 and got trapped in a snowstorm in the Sierra Nevadas. Almost half of the party did not survive.

Gold Is Discovered

When the Bear Flag Revolt broke out, there were about 700 Americans in California. When they learned of the Mexican War, they quickly switched from a bear flag to the American flag. After the war, California became an American territory with a large Mexican population. The population might have stayed that way if a discovery had not taken place on Sutter's property. Sutter had sent a group of men to build a sawmill on the American River and had put James Marshall in charge of the project. While walking down the stream bed on January 24, 1848, Marshall noticed something shiny in the water. It looked like gold. He put it in a sack and took it to Sutter. They tried to keep it a secret, but word leaked out; in May the gold rush began.

The Gold Rush

It took time for word to reach the East, but when President Polk included reports of the gold find in California in a message to Congress, it became official. In 1849, thousands of men kissed their wives and children goodbye and headed for California. There were three basic ways to go: around South America by ship; sail down to Panama, cross the narrow country, and then by ship up to California; or across the continent by land. The most commonly taken route was overland.

Men who had dreams of quick riches were usually disappointed. Prices in California were very high, and chances of finding the "big bonanza" were few; but that did not keep them from coming. Living in nearly all-male camps, working in ice-cold water, and sheltered by a tent or lean-to left many men dreaming of home. Others thought only of the mansion and servants they would have when luck shined on them.

Name: ______________________________ Date: ______________________

The California Gold Rush: Activity

Directions: Use information from the reading selection to complete the graphic organizer

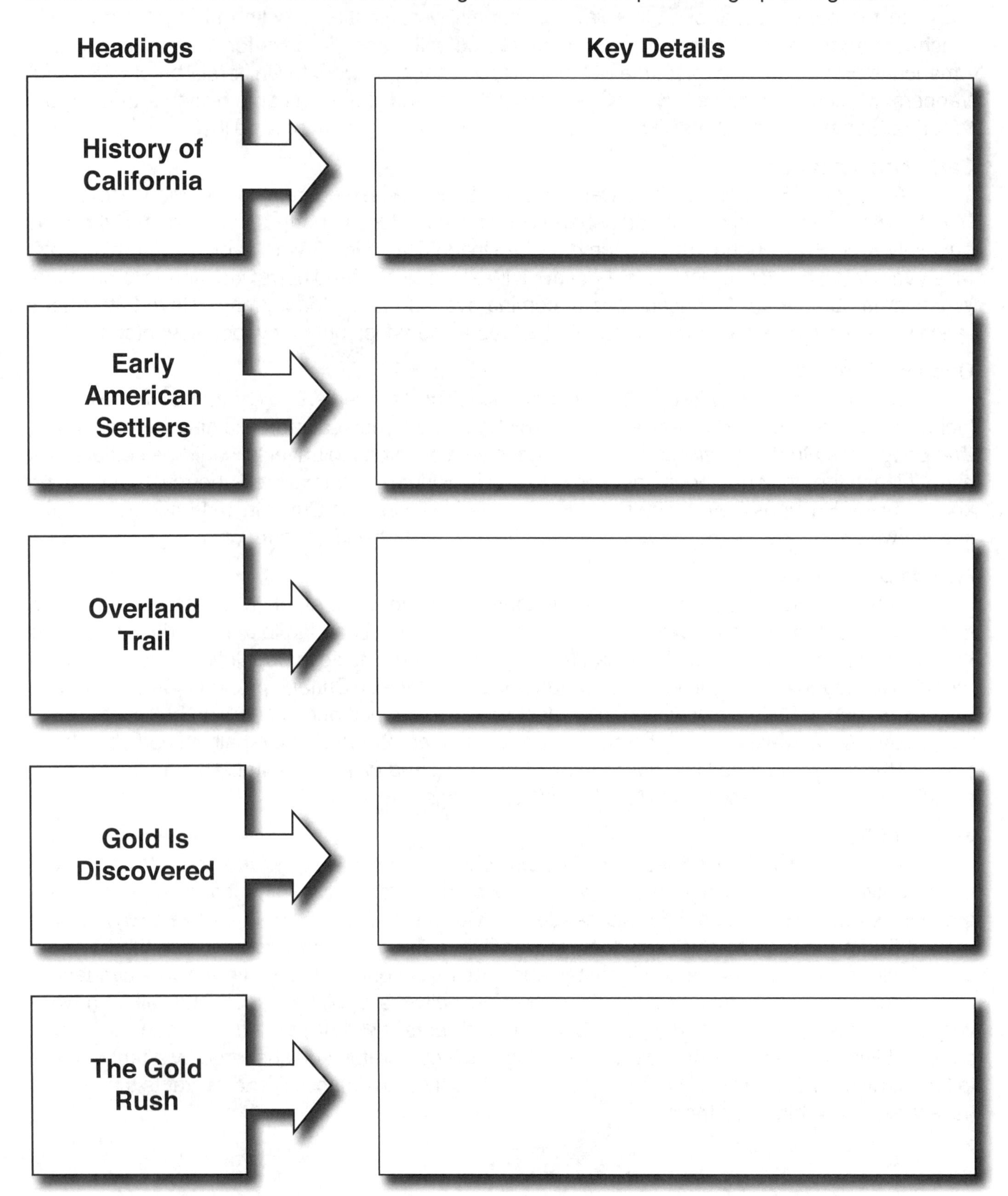

The Compromise of 1850

Daniel Webster

Daniel Webster was the most noted orator, or public speaker, of his time, and whenever he debated, large crowds gathered. When he announced that he would speak on the controversial Compromise of 1850, the nation waited with great interest. Many senators had spoken already: Henry Clay and Stephen Douglas for it, John C. Calhoun against it.

The importance of a speech by Webster would have amazed his early teachers. In school he was good at everything, except public speaking. After graduating from college, he became one of the best-known lawyers in the nation and argued important cases before the Supreme Court. After five years in the House, he became a senator from Massachusetts in 1827. There he had given a dramatic speech against the nullifiers, in which he proclaimed, "Liberty and Union, now and forever, one and inseparable!" While he agreed with Andrew Jackson on the need to keep the Union together, they disagreed strongly on most other issues. He joined with Clay in forming the Whig Party. In 1841, Webster became secretary of state, but in 1844, he returned to the Senate.

Wilmot Proviso

Webster was not enthusiastic about the Mexican War; he thought President Polk should have worked harder on a diplomatic solution. In 1846, the Wilmot Proviso was debated. It forbade slavery in any territory taken from Mexico. Webster supported it because he opposed slavery on moral grounds. The Proviso passed in the House but was defeated because of southern opposition in the Senate.

Slavery and Statehood

With the end of the war and the election of Zachary Taylor as president, the slavery issue was much on Webster's mind. California's gold rush had increased its population enough for it to become a state. To admit California would break the even balance of free and slave states. Other issues were also on people's minds as well. Northern states were passing personal liberty laws making it difficult for slave owners to recapture runaway slaves. Abolitionists opposed the slave trade in the District of Columbia. Texas was in deep debt. The settlers in New Mexico and Utah needed organized government.

Compromise of 1850

Henry Clay put all these issues together in one bill and enlisted help from Senator Stephen Douglas. Known as the Compromise of 1850, it would: (1) admit California as a free state, (2) organize New Mexico and Utah territories and let the people decide whether to be slave or free, (3) legislation, known as the Fugitive Slave Act, was passed to allow for the capture of runaway slaves and return to their owners, (4) end the slave trade in the District of Columbia, and (5) give Texas $10,000,000 in exchange for land in west Texas, which would become part of New Mexico.

On March 7, Webster stood in the Senate and said, "I wish to speak today…as an American…I speak today for the preservation of the Union. Hear me for my cause." For three hours, he spoke of the tensions pulling the nation apart. He said that instead of talking about secession (leaving the Union), Americans should enjoy the "fresh air of liberty and union." His speech helped make compromise possible, but the time for compromises was coming to a close.

Name: ______________________ Date: ______________________

The Compromise of 1850: Activity

Directions: Examine the map below. Then answer the question.

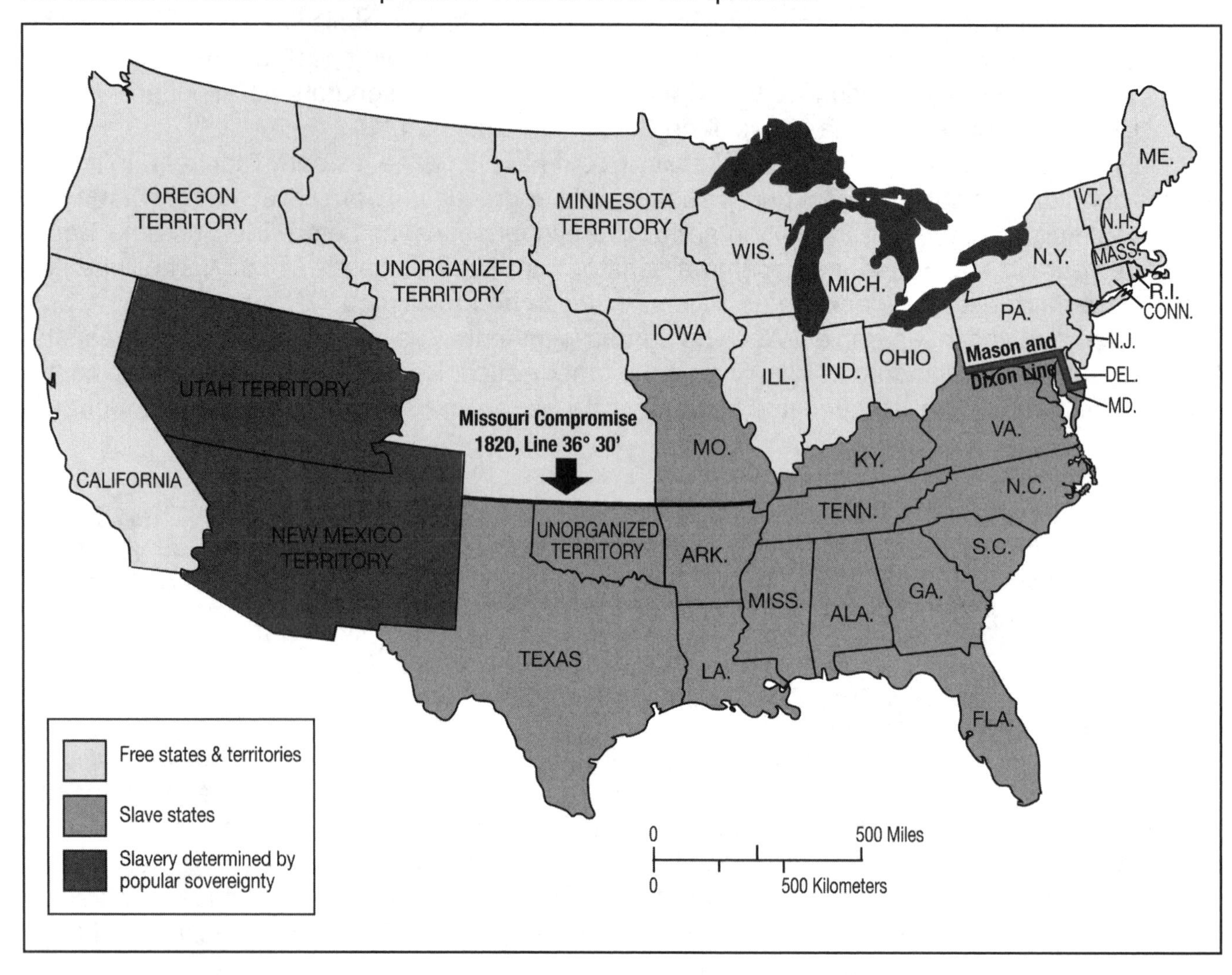

How does the map contribute to your understanding of the Compromise of 1850? Use details from the map to support your answer.

"Bleeding Kansas"

If you were living in 1853, you would never imagine that the newspapers would be full of news about Shawnee Mission, Topeka, Lawrence, and Pottawatomie Creek in the next three years. History is full of such twists of fate, and the impossible becomes reality.

Expansion of Railroads

The reason for Kansas becoming headline news goes back to the rapid growth of California and interest in building a railroad across the continent. A survey had already been run for a railroad from New Orleans to the West Coast, and the Gadsden Purchase made it possible to build that railroad south of the Gila River. Many thought there would be only one railroad, so northern states much preferred a more northern route. As a senator from Illinois, it was logical to Stephen Douglas that it be built west from Chicago. A railroad requires customers in order to be profitable; however, most settlers will not move onto land that has not been surveyed or to areas where there is no government to protect life or property.

Kansas-Nebraska Act

Douglas proposed the Kansas-Nebraska Act in 1854. It provided that Kansas and Nebraska territories be formed and allowed the people who settled there to decide whether or not there would be slavery. This idea was called popular sovereignty. He knew there would be opposition because it would overturn the long-standing Missouri Compromise of 1820, which had blocked any slavery north of 36°30'. Kansas and Nebraska were above that line. Southerners and President Franklin Pierce backed it; many Northerners were opposed. The bill barely passed.

Northerners and Southerners Flock to Kansas

People on both sides realized it was important that their group get control in Kansas. Lying west of Missouri, it might threaten slavery in that state, so Missouri Senator David Atchison urged Southerners to settle there. Many Northerners also saw the importance, and the New England Emigrant Aid Company was formed to help New Englanders settle there. Reverend Henry Ward Beecher, an abolitionist, said that rifles rather than Bibles would determine the issue; and boxes of "Beecher's Bibles" (rifles) were sent to Kansas.

Andrew Reeder was appointed territorial governor. When he called an election, nearly 5,000 Missourians crossed into Kansas and voted. Their vote was enough to win the election, and a pro-slavery legislature was set up at Lecompton. The antislavery people ignored the election and set up their own legislature at Topeka.

Acts of Violence

Acts of violence often took place. Horace Greeley, the publisher of the New York *Tribune,* used the term "Bleeding Kansas" to describe the violence that besieged the territory. On May 21, 1856, a pro-slavery (Border Ruffians) "posse" attacked the antislavery community of Lawrence, threw its printing press into the river, and tore up the town. On May 24, 1856, John Brown, an abolitionist, led a group of men to Pottawatomie Creek, a proslavery town, and killed five men and boys. North and South, Republicans and Democrats watched happenings in Kansas with horror, and each blamed the other for the violence.

Kansas remained tense for years after this, and during the Civil War, trouble often broke out between Missourians and Kansans. In 1861, Kansas was admitted to the Union as a free state.

Name: ______________________ Date: ______________________

"Bleeding Kansas": Activity

Directions: Use the information from the reading selection to complete the graphic organizer.

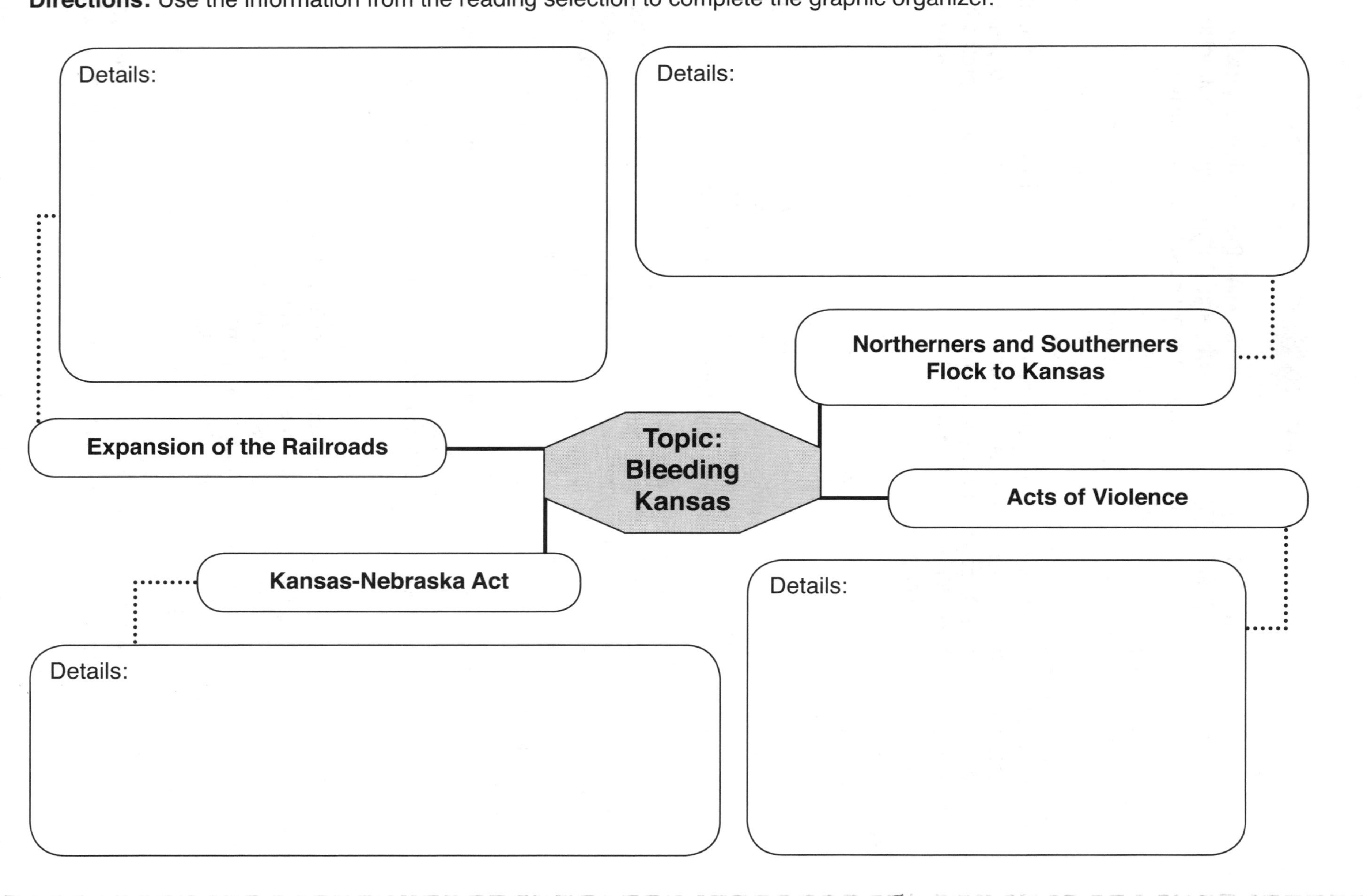

John Brown Attacks Harpers Ferry

John Brown

As John Brown watched the proceedings at his trial, even his friends were making him angry. They tried to defend him by saying he was insane. People had said the same thing about his mother, his aunt, his first wife, and some of his sons. It was the world that was insane, talking about slavery as if it were some legal point, or saying it was a good system or an issue with two sides. To John Brown, slavery was a cause worth dying for. He often quoted the scripture: "Without the shedding of blood, there is no forgiveness of sin."

Slavery was a technical point of law to some. Chief Justice Roger Taney in the *Dred Scott* decision (1857) denied that Congress had any power to keep slavery out of the territories. Debates in Congress, in courts, and in books were mere words. John Brown was not a man of words, but action.

In Kansas, he led the attack on Pottawatomie Creek. After that, he traveled to Boston and talked with abolitionists. Then he returned to Kansas and used it as a base to steal slaves and horses in Missouri. In one raid, he killed a farmer who got in his way. However, a direct blow on slavery was what he really desired. He persuaded some Boston abolitionists, known as the Secret Six, to give him $10,000 for his venture, and he planned his attack on the small, quiet town of Harpers Ferry, Virginia.

Attack on Harpers Ferry

Located on the Potomac River, Harpers Ferry had a federal arsenal, armory, and rifle works; it was also in a slave state. His plan was to arm local slaves, which would signal a general slave rebellion. He and his new army could stay up in the mountains and fight off enemies until victory was won and the last slave was freed. He tried to persuade free African Americans in the North to join him, but they thought the plan was too risky.

On October 16, 1859, Brown's men attacked Harpers Ferry, cut telegraph lines, and stopped the morning train. Men were sent out to bring in slaves from nearby farms and to gather a few white hostages. A freeman who worked for the railroad tried to run away, but he was shot in the back. Brown then allowed the train to leave, and the engineer sent a message that Harpers Ferry was under attack. Colonel Robert E. Lee was sent to Harpers Ferry with some marines. By the time they arrived, Brown's men were in the engine house. After Brown turned down an offer to surrender, the marines attacked and captured the raiders. Ten of Brown's men were killed, including two of his sons.

Sentenced to Death

Brown was charged with murder, inciting slave insurrection, and treason against the state of Virginia. At his trial, he told the court, "Now, if it is deemed necessary that I should forfeit my life for the furtherance of the ends of justice and mingle my blood further with the blood of my children, and with the blood of the millions in this slave country whose rights are disregarded by wicked, cruel, and unjust enactments, I submit. So let it be done." John Brown was found guilty and sentenced to death. He was hanged on December 2, 1859. He became a symbol of self-sacrifice, and as Union soldiers marched, they sang, "John Brown's body lies a-moldering in the grave, as we go marching on."

Name: ______________________________ Date: ______________

John Brown Attacks Harpers Ferry: Activity

Directions: Use the information from the reading selection to complete the newspaper article planner below about John Brown's attack on Harpers Ferry. Use the completed planner to write a newspaper article on a separate sheet of paper or use an online newspaper article generator.

Newspaper Article Planner

Headline: ______________________________

Byline: ______________________________

Lead Paragraph:

Who: ______________________________

What: ______________________________

____

When: ______________________________

Where: ______________________________

Why: ______________________________

____

How: ______________________________

____

Other Facts or Details: ______________________________

____

____

____

____

____

South Carolina Secedes

Across the nation, people gathered at newspaper offices and at the telegraphers' offices in the railroad stations in November 1860. As returns came in, the news was joyous for some, disturbing for some, and grim for others. The reason for all this excitement was the presidential election that had just taken place—one that would have more effect on the future of the nation than any before.

Conventions Elect Their Candidates

The election process had begun in April with a wild Democratic convention in Charleston, South Carolina. The convention produced no harmony and no candidate. Some Southern delegates did everything they could to see that it failed. They reasoned that if the Democrats split, the Republicans would win, and then the South would leave the Union. The Party met again in Baltimore, and again there was trouble. The Southern delegates walked out and chose Senator John Breckinridge of Kentucky as their candidate. Northern delegates chose Senator Stephen Douglas of Illinois.

The Republicans then met in Chicago. Senator William Seward of New York led at first, but on the third ballot, Abraham Lincoln won the nomination. The Republican platform promised homesteads, a railroad to the Pacific, and tariff protection for American industries. On slavery, the platform opposed interference with slavery in the states and called John Brown's raid a crime. In the border states, many did not like any of the choices. They formed the Constitutional Union Party and chose Senator John Bell of Kentucky. They favored the Union and enforcement of the laws.

South Threatens to Secede

During the presidential campaign, Southern newspapers warned that a Lincoln election would result in the South leaving the Union. The Republicans said the South was just repeating the same threats they had used in 1856. In the North, the contest was mostly between Lincoln and Douglas. In the South, it was between Douglas and Breckinridge. In border states from Missouri to Maryland, the strongest support was for Bell or Douglas. In those days, it was considered improper for candidates to go out and give speeches, so campaigns were carried on by big rallies, parades, and speeches by supporters. When it appeared that Lincoln was going to win, Douglas ignored tradition and started campaigning in the South. He urged the South to stay in the Union, regardless of how the election turned out.

Abraham Lincoln Is Elected

Lincoln easily won the election with 180 electoral votes—his opponents, all together, had only 123 (Breckinridge, 72; Bell, 39; Douglas, 12). In popular votes, Lincoln had 1.8 million compared with 2.8 million for all opponents combined. When the news of Lincoln's election reached South Carolina, the legislature called for a convention to decide whether the state should secede, leave the Union. Six other states prepared to hold conventions after South Carolina acted. On December 20, 1860, South Carolina voted to leave the Union. In other states of the Deep South, this was a signal to act. South Carolina, by its own action, was now an "independent nation." It was not alone for long, however. Six states joined it, and in a meeting in Montgomery, Alabama, the Confederate States of America was formed. Jefferson Davis was elected provisional president. Everyone waited now to see how Lincoln would react.

Name: ______________________________ Date: ______________________

South Carolina Secedes: Activity

Directions: Use the information from the reading selection to answer the questions.

1. What happened at the Democratic Convention?

2. What happened at the Republican Convention?

3. What was Stephen Douglas's view on secession?

4. What was the South's reaction to news of Lincoln's election?

Lincoln Asks for 75,000 Volunteers

March 4, 1861, finally arrived, and for tired, worn President Buchanan, it was not quickly enough. Seven states had left the Union and had formed the Confederacy (CSA). U.S. forts and arsenals were taken by the states, and Southern militia units were drilling on a regular basis. Only Fort Sumter in Charleston harbor and Fort Pickens off the Florida coast remained in U.S. hands. Still, no one knew whether there would be a war. Some in the North were willing to let the South go peacefully, but no one was sure what President-elect Abraham Lincoln would do. On his trip from Springfield, Illinois, to Washington, D.C., he made no statement hinting at what his policy would be. The nation waited nervously to see if Lincoln's policy would bring peace or war.

Lincoln's Inaugural Address

In words carefully chosen, Lincoln said in his inaugural address, "In *your* hands, my dissatisfied fellow countrymen, and not in *mine,* is the momentous issue of civil war. The government will not assail *you.* You can have no conflict without being yourselves the aggressors." In other words, there would not be a war unless the South started it.

Battle of Fort Sumter

The nation's attention focused on Fort Sumter, commanded by Colonel Robert Anderson from Kentucky. He had quietly removed the small garrison from Fort Moultrie, across the harbor from Fort Sumter, but he knew that unless food and other supplies were sent, he could not hold out for long. A relief ship, *Star of the West,* had tried to reach Fort Sumter in January but had turned back after being hit by South Carolina militia cannons. No further effort was made to send supplies by President Buchanan. The new Confederate government sent General P.G.T. Beauregard to Charleston to take command. By the time Lincoln became president, Fort Sumter was almost out of food. To supply the fort meant certain war; not to supply it would be to hand it over without a fight. When Beauregard sent officers to the fort, Anderson told them he could not hold out much longer, but the South knew relief ships were on the way. On April 12, 1861, Confederate guns opened fire on Fort Sumter, and two days later, Anderson surrendered. The Confederate flag flew over the fort, and Anderson and his men were allowed to leave.

Lincoln Acts and States React

Lincoln acted quickly and called on the nation's governors to send 75,000 militia to serve three-month terms as federal soldiers. In border states, governors were put on the spot. In the states of the Upper South (Virginia, Tennessee, North Carolina, and Arkansas), the governors said they would never think of fighting their friends to the South, and they and their states left the Union. Missouri's governor wanted to secede, but the Union army chased him and his friends out of the state. Maryland also had strong Southern sentiment, but federal troops took control. Kentucky was so divided that it decided to stay neutral and warned both sides against sending an army into the state. Delaware was Unionist all the way.

Robert E. Lee Offers His Services to the Confederacy

As states decided which way to go, individuals also made decisions. For Colonel Robert E. Lee, deciding was especially painful. He did not approve of slavery or secession. He was offered command of the U.S. Army but turned it down. He was a Virginian, and when his state left the Union, he and many like him offered their services to the Confederacy.

Name: ______________________________ Date: ____________________

Lincoln Asks for 75,000 Volunteers: Activity

Directions: The chart contains the first four paragraphs of a proclamation issued by Abraham Lincoln on April 15, 1861. Paraphrase, or restate in your own words, each paragraph.

April 15, 1861, Declaration	Paraphrase (restate in your own words)
(1) WHEREAS the laws of the United States have been, for some time past, and now are opposed, and the execution thereof obstructed, in the States of South Carolina, Georgia, Alabama, Florida, Mississippi, Louisiana, and Texas, by combinations too powerful to be suppressed by the ordinary course of judicial proceedings, or by the powers vested in the marshals by law:	
(2) Now, therefore, I, ABRAHAM LINCOLN, President of the United States, in virtue of the power in me vested by the Constitution and the laws, have thought fit to call forth, and hereby do call forth, the militia of the several States of the Union, to the aggregate number of seventy-five thousand, in order to suppress said combinations, and to cause the laws to be duly executed. The details for this object will be immediately communicated to the State authorities through the War Department	
(3) I appeal to all loyal citizens to favor, facilitate, and aid this effort to maintain the honor, the integrity, and the existence of our National Union, and the perpetuity of popular government; and to redress wrongs already long enough endured.	
(4) I deem it proper to say that the first service assigned to the forces hereby called forth will probably be to repossess the forts, places, and property which have been seized from the Union; and in every event, the utmost care will be observed, consistently with the objects aforesaid, to avoid any devastation, any destruction of, or interference with, property, or any disturbance of peaceful citizens in any part of the country.	

African Americans and the War Effort

In 1861, the free black population was about 500,000 in the United States; almost half of the population was living in the North. Among them was Frederick Douglass, who had escaped from slavery. Others were freed by their masters, bought freedom, came north over the Underground Railroad, or were born in the North. Most of them lived in cities and had developed churches, clubs, and schools. Education was very important to them, and some even attended college. In the South, some freemen were prosperous, but most free blacks in both the North and South were poor. They all knew they would never feel free until slavery was no more.

Abraham Lincoln

Lincoln agreed that slavery should end, but he resisted pressures by abolitionists and freemen to be rushed into acting too soon. He faced several complicated problems.

- **Primary Objective:** To him, the question of freeing slaves was less important than saving the Union. If the South won the war, slavery would go on as before.
- **Military:** Four border slave states had remained in the Union: Missouri, Maryland, Kentucky, and Delaware. By acting too soon, opinion in those states would turn against the Union. If they left the Union, the war could be lost.
- **Legal:** The Constitution said that private property could not be taken without just compensation to the owner. He tried to talk some slave state leaders into giving up slavery in return for $400 per slave. They turned him down.

"Contraband of War"

Meanwhile, African Americans were helping the war effort on both sides. In the South, they produced food, acted as servants for soldiers, and built fortifications. In the North, free black men wanted to enlist in the army but were turned down. However, officers in the field began using runaway slaves as workers. General Ben Butler called them "contraband of war," and after that, they were often referred to as "contrabands."

Preliminary Emancipation Proclamation Issued

Waiting until after the North won a major battle in 1862 (so it would not look like a desperate measure), Lincoln issued a preliminary Emancipation Proclamation, saying that on January 1, 1863, "All persons held as slaves within any state [still in rebellion] shall be…forever free." Since the South was using slaves in its war effort, he justified ending slavery as a war measure. It did not satisfy some abolitionists, and it angered the South.

African-American Soldiers

Some Union officers began enlisting African-American soldiers before it was government policy. The first unit officially approved was the 1st South Carolina Volunteers commanded by Colonel Thomas Higginson. It was made up of escaped slaves from the South. The 54th Massachusetts Volunteer Infantry Regiment, led by Colonel Robert Shaw, was the first military unit of African-American soldiers created in the North.

African-American soldiers were paid less than whites, were often used as labor details, and were the most poorly equipped. Despite this, desertions were very rare, and they performed well in battle. In 1863 at Fort Wagner, South Carolina, 247 of Shaw's men were killed out of the unit's 600 men. Sixteen African-American soldiers received the Congressional Medal of Honor.

Confederate Major General Patrick Cleburne suggested in 1863 that slaves be recruited. The idea was turned down at the time, but in 1865, General Lee suggested it, and his idea was accepted. By that time, however, the war was lost.

Name: ______________________________ Date: ______________________

African Americans and the War Effort: Activity

Directions: Circle T if the statement is true or F if the statement is false.

T F 1. In 1861, the free black population in the United States was less than 300,000.

T F 2. Fredrick Douglass was born a freeman.

T F 3. Most free African Americans in the North lived in cities.

T F 4. Lincoln resisted pressure from the abolitionists to immediately end slavery.

T F 5. Lincoln's primary objective was to end slavery in the South.

T F 6. Missouri, Maryland, Kentucky, and Delaware were border states that did not secede from the Union.

T F 7. African Americans assisted the war effort on both sides.

T F 8. Runaway slaves were often referred to as "contrabands."

T F 9. On January 1, 1863, Lincoln issued a preliminary Emancipation Proclamation.

T F 10. The first officially approved African-American military unit was the 1st South Carolina Volunteers.

T F 11. The 54th Massachusetts unit lost 247 men at the Battle of Fort Wagner.

T F 12. Afrian-American soldiers were not allowed to receive the Congressional Medial of Honor.

T F 13. All Civil War soldiers received equal pay.

T F 14. Desertion was a rare occurrence for African-American soldiers.

T F 15. In 1865, General Robert E. Lee suggested recruiting African-American soldiers for the South.

A Time of Southern Victories

Statistics seemed to show that the Confederacy did not have any chance of winning the Civil War. They were outnumbered 10–1 in manufacturing, 3–1 in miles of railroad, and 2–1 in manpower. Their roads and railroads were much worse than those in the North. Despite the odds, the South thought they could win. At times, it looked as if they might be able to win just enough so the North would give them independence.

Robert E. Lee

The South had a few things going for it. Most of the time, Southerners were fighting on familiar land with many civilians keeping them informed on what the Union Army was doing. They also had many fine officers who had been trained at West Point and southern military schools. Among these were Robert E. Lee, Thomas (Stonewall) Jackson, Joseph Johnston, James Longstreet, and J.E.B. Stuart. At the beginning of the war, both armies were almost equally armed and neither had previous battlefield experience.

Battle of Bull Run (First Manassas)

After the attack on Fort Sumter in April 1861, both sides raised large armies. Commanding the North's Army of the Potomac was General Irwin McDowell; the South's Army of Northern Virginia was led by General P.G.T. Beauregard. The two armies met at Bull Run near Manassas, Virginia, and it seemed like a Union victory until Stonewall Jackson's fresh Confederate troops arrived. The Union army broke under the pressure and rushed back to Washington. The Southern troops did not pursue, which made President Jefferson Davis angry.

Generals are Replaced

McDowell was replaced by General George McClellan, a careful man who did not want to fight until victory was certain. Rather than move by land toward Richmond, he transported his army by boat to the James Peninsula, southeast of Richmond. The Confederate general preparing to defend the city was Joe Johnston. When Johnston was wounded, General Robert E. Lee replaced him. Lee sent Jackson toward the North to keep Lincoln from sending more men to McClellan. Jackson's men moved so fast that they were known as "foot cavalry," and that caused Union troops to be sent after him. Lee then attacked in the Seven Days' Campaign. As McClellan left the Peninsula, Lee had to turn quickly to face a new army, that of John Pope. The two armies fought the Second Battle of Bull Run, and again the South won.

McClellan was again appointed commander of the Union army. Lee's army moved north into western Maryland. After Union soldiers found a copy of Lee's orders wrapped around three cigars, McClellan sent his army to meet the Confederates at Antietam Creek. In a bloody battle that left 25,000 men dead or wounded, the Confederates withdrew across the Potomac River to Virginia. Because McClellan did not attack Lee's army as they retreated, McClellan was fired. General Ambrose Burnside replaced him.

Burnside planned to move quickly across the Rappahannock River at Fredericksburg, but the pontoons he needed for the bridge did not arrive when they were expected. When they did cross the river, the Confederates were well prepared, and the Union soldiers were badly beaten. Joe Hooker replaced Burnside, and the two armies met again at Chancellorsville. In a daring move, Lee split his outnumbered army and hit Hooker's flank. The Union Army headed north in defeat.

Name: ______________________________ Date: ____________________

A Time of Southern Victories: Activity

Directions: Find and circle the words listed below related to the A Time of Southern Victories reading selection. Words may be printed forward, backward, horizontally, vertically, or diagonally.

```
L L G Z S R Y J X V S H Z A D D B Z X D J H W W B I Y S Y F
A E Q W Q H N N A I O A B S E Z D L W T N P T J K S B K T L
X B F I G V P J U N C D F G C J G W I Q N T W Z A F K G V U
Z G R B S H C K O T Q O V I B W P G Z V R E O O R E A N D J
J Z Y A Z A V O Q E M X X M U S L G U U S W L S E O Q R A D
O O B J H R L I Q S H F M E J M C L Z T C A X R Q M C M F S
L L S A X A Y T D W A O P P X Y B U K V O S C F M P E J E B
S J O E T K M S X B W D O Y U S I P P S L M J U D S C C I R
A E I U P T B L F B F G A K N V W X K N A Z K J L O L A O D
D R Z D Y H L G I O T F F I E G C Z X T T O K O K E L B P N
P X R K I Z J E M N Z K D B L R I L E J D T N T B C E P Z U
D G I O G I W O O N C E O J Q P W I O R K G W T J R D Z P R
K T T W B J X O H F C O Y D Q H T N F A S L O C T X V W S L
S I W B N Z X F W N B N L X M N E A C T Z X Z E I K Z S N L
Y E S Q E J Q V O J S U N N A S R T R I E X L M Q G M T L U
J L E C K A E Z W X O T L T C R C E B M V E J T N V E O W B
D L E A S V U B I O G E O L N C E L I F E Z Y A M D O N M F
U I P A F I G R S Z G Q J N R T Y I P F C T L V I A P E D O
Z V O J D K V V E T U T O E Z U Q G S G N L Q S Z Q H W G E
V S P S Z O X A P G U C R I I P N G K X E I N I E D Z A L L
F R N N A Z U O D C A A D B R X F R Y L A R T L R N L L X T
I O H S A M B N A N G R R N M Z E T C D U V B W E Y P L L T
Z L O U X J E S I O O V D T C A M C H B Y T J P T A V J P A
E L J E N C J E N K A S Z L Q L M M E V S B S D M J L A G B
K E A W A H J V S R P Y R T I E H S F D C Z C I U T Y C E D
Y C T P T T W E P M R J F E G Z O I P N Q F Q E S V V K L N
E N Q C O R O N A E W G Q R F R I B Z X B L W M T A Q S K O
B A S Z D Z D T O N D V O J B F R L W A C R V G R K D O M C
M H E Z S V P N T X S E C M C T E J B Z R D O E O H A N O E
I C H B T H Z W Q L G W A S K Z A J D D N F H U F G C G D S
```

ABRAHAM LINCOLN
AMBROSE BURNSIDE
ANTIETAM CREEK
BATTLE OF BULL RUN
CHANCELLORSVILLE
FORT SUMTER
GEORGE MCCLELLAN
JAMES LONGSTREET
J.E.B. STUART
JEFFERSON DAVIS
JOE HOOKER
JOHN POPE
JOSEPH JOHNSTON
P.G.T. BEAUREGARD
ROBERT E. LEE
STONEWALL JACKSON
SECOND BATTLE OF BULL RUN

July 4, 1863—A Day of Northern Victories

General Grant

While much of the nation's attention was on Union defeats in Virginia, Ulysses Grant, a Union general in the West, was gaining a reputation for winning. Grant was a West Point graduate who was appointed a colonel in the Illinois infantry when the war began, but he soon showed an ability to win battles. Victories at Fort Henry and Fort Donelson gave the Union control of the Tennessee River. Lincoln made Grant a major general. In April 1862 during the Battle of Shiloh, Grant was able to take an army that had been badly mauled, turn it around, and win. In each of these battles, the navy helped him.

Vicksburg

Grant's next assignment was much more difficult—to capture the city of Vicksburg, Mississippi. It sat on a high bluff on the Mississippi River. If Vicksburg fell, it would divide the western and eastern parts of the Confederacy. However, it could not be approached without the Confederates knowing about it. The Union had been trying to capture it since the spring of 1862.

In April 1863, Grant moved his army southward into Louisiana on the west side of the river. A fleet under Admiral David Porter blasted its way past the Confederate batteries (heavy guns) at Vicksburg and joined Grant far south of Vicksburg. During the night of April 30, protected by gunboats, Grant's army crossed into Mississippi. Throughout May, Grant won battles at Port Gibson, Raymond, Jackson (the capital city), and Champion Hill. Confederate General John Pemberton was forced to retreat to Vicksburg. Grant then turned westward to attack Vicksburg from the rear. By May 25, the city of Vicksburg was besieged by Union forces. Exploding shells forced residents to live in caves, and food supplies ran low. Finally, on July 4, 1863, General Pemberton surrendered, and 30,000 Confederate soldiers were captured.

Gettysburg

In 1863, the Confederate government approved General Robert E. Lee's plan to invade Pennsylvania. It might relieve pressure on Vicksburg, encourage the northern peace movement, and feed the army at the North's expense. The army had been so successful that any doubts were removed that they could go all the way to Harrisburg and even capture Washington, D.C. With 75,000 men, the Confederate Army of Northern Virginia headed northward.

On June 28, 1863, Lincoln replaced General Joe Hooker with General George Meade as the commander of the Union Army. By then, Southern troops had reached Chambersburg and York and were near Harrisburg. No one planned to fight at Gettysburg, but on July 1, Confederate troops met strong resistance there, and messages were sent by both sides to their commanders. Troops were rushed to this quiet town, and the greatest battle ever fought in North America was underway.

At Gettysburg, the Union Army held Cemetery Ridge, and Lee was determined to drive them off. The greatest effort took place on July 3, when 15,000 men crossed the field toward the Union line in the famous Pickett's Charge. About 7,000 men were lost in the attempt. On July 4, General Lee expected the North to attack, but when nothing happened, he began his retreat. Because of high water, he could not cross the Potomac River until July 13. The next day, General Meade attacked, but it was too late to do much harm because most of the Confederates were already across the river. The Confederates were badly bruised, but still dangerous. General Meade's failure to capture General Lee and his army contributed to the war continuing for nearly two more years, but the South had lost too many men to ever again take the offensive.

Name: ______________________________ Date: ______________________

July 4, 1863—A Day of Northern Victories: Activity

Directions: Answer the following questions. Support your answers with information from the reading selection.

1. Why was it important for the Union to capture Vicksburg?

2. What were General Lee's motives for invading Pennsylvania?

3. Why do you think General Lee retreated from Gettysburg?

4. What was the result of General Meade's failure to capture General Lee and his army?

Women Join the War Effort on Both Sides

As Civil War soldiers went off to war, they often sang of "The Girl I Left Behind." Love ballads like "Lorena" and "Aura Lee" were popular with both armies in the Civil War. It was Julia Ward Howe who inspired Union troops with her song, "The Battle Hymn of the Republic."

Women on the Home Front

Women were not supposed to be part of war, but they were as patriotic and enthusiastic as the men. John Milton had written: "They also serve who only stand and wait." These women were determined to do more than stand and wait. They would help. Women took over the farms, doing the chores their husbands had always done. Women went to work in factories to produce arms and clothing needed by the armies. Before this time, it had not been proper for a "lady" to do much of the work that necessity now required.

Women Spies

Some women became active participants in the war. Women spies were used by both sides, and some became famous. Rose Greenhow lived in Washington and knew many government officials. She sent General Beauregard word that the Union Army was moving toward Bull Run. She was captured and held prisoner for a while. Belle Boyd often went through Union lines carrying information to Stonewall Jackson and medicine for his troops. She was arrested six times and put in prison twice. During the war, many other women reported Union troop movements to Confederate officers. A few women even disguised themselves as men and enlisted in the army.

Of Northern spies, the most important was Elizabeth Van Lew, who lived in Richmond and gathered information from Union prisoners held at Libby Prison. She was even able to plant one of her former slaves, Mary Bowser, as a servant at Jefferson Davis's home. Her information to General Grant was very useful, and when his army entered Richmond, he stopped at her home for tea.

Women Serve as Nurses

Taking care of the soldiers' needs was a common activity of women. Those in Richmond often opened their homes to soldiers in need of a home-cooked meal. After a battle, homes in the area became field hospitals for wounded and sick soldiers. Nursing wounded soldiers was a common activity among Southern women during the war. Because the South was short on medical supplies, food, and doctors, women were crucial in the saving of many lives. Some Northern women were best known for their role in nursing. Dorothea Dix was Superintendent of United States Army Nurses, with a rank equal to that of a major general. When she saw the needs of soldiers, she issued appeals for bed shirts, preserves, and canned goods. Every request she made for supplies was more than met by donations from all over the North. She came down on hospital superintendents who mistreated the men. Clara Barton became famous as a battlefield nurse. She later founded the American Red Cross. Mary "Mother" Bickerdyke was a widow in her forties who devoted great efforts to taking care of enlisted men. General Grant and General Sherman admired her efforts.

What Were the Results?

Women made important contributions to the war effort in both the North and the South. For the first time, women began to experience a sense of independence and accomplishment that would not be forgotten after the war. Women were beginning to see that they could make valuable contributions to their families and the nation in careers outside the home.

Name: ______________________ Date: ______________

Women Join the War Effort on Both Sides: Activity

Directions: Use the information from the reading selection to complete the graphic organizer.

Central Idea: Women made important contributions to the war effort in both the North and South.

Women on the Home Front	Women Spies	Women Serve as Nurses
Main Idea:	**Main Idea:**	**Main Idea:**
Details	**Details**	**Details**

President Lincoln Is Assassinated

After defeats at Vicksburg and Gettysburg, friends of the South watched events unfold with greater gloom. Grant went on to defeat the South at Chattanooga and was then appointed supreme commander of Union forces. He took command of the Army of the Potomac and assigned General William T. Sherman the task of marching to Atlanta and then from Atlanta to the coast. When General Joe Johnston could not stop the advance, President Davis replaced him with General John Hood. Hood lost Atlanta in September 1864, and Sherman made a path 60 miles wide to the coast, arriving in Savannah on December 22, 1864. The South, divided at the Mississippi in 1863, had been divided again. Meanwhile, Grant was conducting a relentless campaign that began with the Wilderness in May 1864; ignoring enormous losses, he pinned Lee's army down in the trenches at Petersburg, Virginia.

Lincoln Is Reelected

Also devastating to Confederate supporters was Lincoln's reelection in 1864. During the war, a group of Democrats called "Copperheads" tried to stir up opposition to the war and to Lincoln. They had counted on the 1864 election as a way for those who did not like the war, the draft, the Emancipation Proclamation, or Lincoln to defeat him by electing George McClellan. When Lincoln won, most accepted it. John Wilkes Booth did not, however.

John Wilkes Booth

Booth was the son of famous actor Junius Booth and grew up in an acting family. John Wilkes wasn't as impressed with the lines of Shakespeare's plays as with the action. In sword-fighting scenes, he was so intense that he often injured his opponent. He sometimes leaped from boulders on the stage to give greater effect. He loved plays with sinister plots and high drama. He was popular with the ladies and with a strange assortment of admiring misfits. Among these were Lewis Powell and George Atzerodt, known to be "a notorious coward."

When Booth was unhappy, he drank; and as news of Confederate defeats came, he was more despondent than ever. He loved the South and felt a need to do something desperate and theatrical to save it. He had plotted a kidnapping of Lincoln in the past, but his plans never worked out. Lee's surrender at Appomattox Court House on April 9, 1865, made kidnapping useless. Booth had heard Lincoln's brief and conciliatory speech at the White House on April 11 and vowed, "That is the last speech he will ever make." His thoughts now turned to murder.

Assassination at Ford's Theatre

On April 14, 1865, Booth learned that Lincoln would attend Ford's Theatre that evening, and he called his friends together. Atzerodt was to kill Vice President Andrew Johnson, Powell was to kill Secretary of State Seward, and Booth would kill Lincoln. Atzerodt did nothing, but Powell broke into Seward's home and attacked him in his bed. However, Booth would have to play the leading role himself.

Sneaking into Lincoln's box at Ford's Theatre, Booth shot Lincoln in the head. In the leap from the box to the stage, his spur caught in the bunting, and he landed off-balance, breaking his leg. Shouting *"Sic semper tyrannis,"* which means "thus always to tyrants," Booth left the stage and rode off into the night.

President Lincoln was carefully carried across the street to a nearby boarding house. Lincoln never regained consciousness. He died the following morning. On April 26, Booth was surrounded in a barn near Port Royal, Virginia. He was shot and died a few hours later.

Name: ______________________________ Date: ____________________

President Lincoln Is Assassinated: Activity

On April 14, 1865, President Lincoln was shot by John Wilkes Booth. He was carefully carried unconscious to a nearby boarding house where Dr. C. S. Taft attended him. Dr. Taft kept a detailed record of Lincoln's injuries and care until his death.

Directions: Go online to the web address below and read the journal entries of Dr. Taft. Record the key details concerning Dr. Taft's care of President Lincoln. Then write a summary.

Web Address:
<http://digital.library.mcgill.ca/lincoln/exhibit/imgdisplay.php?item=3&sec=4&taft=>

Key Detail

Key Detail

Key Detail

Key Detail

Summary

____
____
____
____
____
____
____
____
____
____
____
____
____
____

Key Detail

Key Detail

Key Detail

Key Detail

Answer Keys

Queen Isabella and Christopher Columbus: Activity (p. 6)

Experience 1: He was interested in sailing at "an early age," and had gone to sea by the age of 15.

Experience 2: In Portugal, he learned valuable skills: reading, writing, navigation, and seamanship.

Experience 3: In the Atlantic, he practiced skills needed for open-ocean sailing.

Experience 4: He took voyages to the Canary Islands and the African Gold Coast where he learned about trade winds.

Captain John Smith and Jamestown: Activity (p. 8)

(Answers will vary but may include:)

Event: John Smith was captured by the Turks and held as a slave, but escaped and returned to England.

Event: He was captured by the Powhatan tribe, but his life was spared by the interference of the chief's daughter, Pocahontas.

Event: He was arrested for the deaths of the two men who went with him on his adventures into Powhatan territory. He was found innocent and later elected council president of Jamestown.

The Pilgrims and the Puritans: Activity (p. 10)

Activity 1

Alike: originally Catholic; unhappy with the Church of England; disliked the king assuming the power of the pope; followed the teaching of John Calvin

Different: Puritans: wanted to purify the church by removing all statues, bishops and rituals. Pilgrims: wanted to separate completely from the Anglican or new church.

Activity 2

The importance of the Mayflower Compact was its provisions, such as people agreeing to form a civil body ruled by laws passed by the majority. The provisions served as examples for future constitutions.

The French and Indian War Begins: Activity (p. 12)

(Answers may vary.)

Reason: The British were used to meeting their enemy in open fields, unlike Native Americans who concealed themselves behind trees in thick forests.

Reason: By marching in rows, many British soldiers could be killed at one time by their enemy.

Reason: The British soldiers dressed in red uniforms, making them stand out in their surroundings

Reason: The British were not used to fighting in all types of weather.

New Laws Anger Colonists: Activity (p. 14)

Navigation Acts: controlled colonial trade and authorized the collection of taxes in the colonies on non-English imports.

Reaction: Colonists rarely thought about the laws since the laws weren't enforced before the war.

Writs of Assistance: allowed any government official to search homes of colonists.

Reaction: Colonists began to understand their liberty was in danger of being lost.

Stamp Act: required a revenue stamp be placed on legal documents, newspapers, and marriage licenses.

Reaction: Men and boys formed a group called the Sons of Liberty, who engaged in protest activities.

Quartering Act: required colonists to provide housing for British soldiers sent to protect them.

Reaction: The colonists did not want the soldiers in their homes.

Declaratory Act: declared England had every right to make any law for the colonies they chose.

Reaction: Colonists paid no attention to the law, but it would lead to future trouble.

Sam Adams—Rabble Rouser (p. 16)

(Answers will vary but may include:)

Event 1: Parliament passed the Townshend Acts.

Event 2: The soldiers reacted by firing and killing four civilians (called the Boston Massacre).

Event 3: Protesters dumped tea in Boston Harbor.

Event 4: The British closed the Port of Boston, put Massachusetts under a military governor, and forced colonists to house British soldiers in their homes. Americans united against these laws.

Patrick Henry: Activity (p. 18)

Statement 1: If protecting the rights of the colonists was considered an act of treason, then they should go ahead and do whatever else they needed to do to protect their rights.

Statement 2: The colonists needed to identify themselves as part of a united group (Americans) instead of a member of an individual colony (Virginia).

Statement 3: Is the price of life and peace worth the cost of being ruled by the British?

Statement 4: I don't care what anyone else does, but I am choosing liberty even if it costs me my life.

The Declaration of Independence: Activity (p. 20)

September 1774: First Continental Congress meets

April 19, 1775: Battle at Lexington and Concord

May 1775: Second Continental Congress meets

June 11, 1776: Committee appointed to draft the Declaration of Independence

July 4, 1776: The Declaration of Independence is adopted.

Americans Fight for Liberty: Activity (p. 22)

1. title; headings; boldface print; sidebar
2. description or chronological/sequential

3. to inform
4. and 5. Answers will vary.

Benedict Arnold—Traitor: Activity (p. 24)
(Answers will vary but may include:)
Details: overlooked for promotion to major general; his help not mentioned in General Gate's official report about the Battle of Saratoga; married an English sympathizer; fell into heavy debt after marriage

Treaty of Paris: Activity (p. 26)
Event 1: Franklin gained France's support in the form of loans, grants, and secret supply shipments.
Event 2: France officially recognized the independence of the United States from Britain.
Event 3: France agreed to join the fight on the side of the Americans.
Event 4: The fighting was officially ended. The United States gained land west to the Mississippi River, Florida was given back to Spain, and the property of Loyalists seized during the war was to be returned.

Articles of Confederation: Activity (p. 28)
Powers: declare war and peace; manage foreign affairs; maintain an army and navy; issue and borrow money; deal with the Native Americans
Weaknesses: no president or executive; no power to tax; states failed to support new government; members of Congress did not take their responsibilities seriously; Congress had no power to enforce peace treaty; states weren't unified, increasing likelihood of foreign involvement; Congress was unable to pay back wages of soldiers

Old Soldiers Threaten Civilian Rule: Activity (p. 30)
(Answers will vary but may include:)
soldiers who couldn't pay their debts were placed in debtor prison; meeting of discontented officers was held; court seized property of farmers who had not paid taxes; Shays led farmers in a rebellion; some state militias revolted; worthless paper money was issued by some states

The Constitutional Convention: Activity (p. 32)
1781: thirteen independent states unified under one government
1785: worked on trade problems on the Potomac River; decided to hold a meeting in Annapolis with all 13 states to discuss problems with trade
1786: worked on trade problems among the states; decided to hold a meeting in Philadelphia to address the defects in the Articles of Confederation
1787: decided to write a new constitution; after debate and compromise, produced the Constitution of the United States

George Washington Becomes President: Activity (p. 34)
1. O 2. O 3. F 4. F 5. F 6. O
7. F 8. F 9. F 10. F 11. O 12. F

Eli Whitney Invents the Cotton Gin: Activity (p. 36)
(Answers will vary but may include:)
Positive Consequences: sped up process of separating seed from cotton; one person could do in one day what previously had taken months to complete; increased cotton production; made cotton cloth more affordable
Negative Consequences: slavery expanded as the need for more workers increased; price of slaves increased; no incentive for South to end slavery

The Alien and Sedition Acts: Activity (p. 38)
alien: not a citizen of the country in which they are dwelling
sedition: promoting discontent against a government
Federalist: a member of a former political party in the United States that favored a strong centralized federal government
resolution: a formal agreement that has been voted on by a group

The Louisiana Purchase: Activity (p. 40)
(Details will vary.)
Central Idea: The Louisiana Purchase allowed for the expansion of the United States.
Detail: gained 827,000 square miles of land
Detail: allowed the U. S. borders to expand to the crest of the Rocky Mountains
Detail: gave U.S. authority over New Orleans, a trading hub
Detail: provided a new source for mineral rights and agricultural development
Summary: The Louisiana Purchase allowed for the expansion of the United States. The U.S. gained 827,000 square miles of land. It allowed the U. S. borders to expand to the crest of the Rocky Mountains. The U.S. gained authority over New Orleans, a trading hub. The new land provided a source for mineral rights and agricultural development.

***Marbury v. Madison:* Activity (p. 42)**
Event 1: Chief Justice of the Supreme Court that decided the *Marbury v. Madison* case
Event 2: defined the membership of a circuit court (2 Supreme Court Justices and 1 district judge)
Event 3: led to the filing of the lawsuit known as *Marbury v. Madison*
Event 4: established the principal of judicial review; gave the court power to declare an act of Congress invalid (Marbury lost, and the Judiciary Act of 1789 was declared unconstitutional.)

Robert Fulton and the Steamboat: Activity (p. 44)

1. made his own pencils; invented a skyrocket; devised a manually powered paddlewheel for his fishing boat
2. worked on a system of lifting boats over difficult spots in canals; invented a dredging machine for cutting canal channels
3. built a submarine; invented an underwater mine, called a coffer; designed a steam warship
4. built the *Clermont,* the first commercially successful steamboat; the *New Orleans* was the first steamboat to travel down the Ohio and Mississippi Rivers; designed a steam warship

Events Leading Up to the War of 1812: Activity (p. 46)

1. The British were stopping and searching American ships for deserters. In addition to deserters, they took crewmen who looked strong and impressed them into British service. If the men complained they risked flogging.
2. The British ship the *Leopard* opened fire on the U.S. Navy ship the *Chesapeake.* The *Chesapeake* surrendered, and the British impressed four *Chesapeake* crewmen.
3. The guns left behind by Native Americans after the battle bore English markings. American westerners felt this proved the British were supplying the natives with arms.

The Missouri Compromise of 1820: Activity (p. 48)

<u>James Tallmadge</u>: proposed an amendment to an enabling act allowing for the formation of state governments for Maine and Missouri. The amendment stated "no more slaves could be taken to Missouri" and slaves born in Missouri to slave parents were to be freed at the age of 25.

<u>Jesse Thomas</u>: offered a compromise to Tallmadge's amendment. It stated Missouri would enter the Union as a slave state and Maine as a free state.

<u>Henry Clay</u>: helped pass a resolution stating, "Missouri must never use its power to take away the rights of an American citizen."

The Election of 1824: Activity (p. 50)

1. The Twelfth Amendment said the "president and vice president were to be chosen by separate ballots. If no one had a majority of votes, the House would choose the president from among the top three candidates, and the Senate would choose the vice president from the top two." In the Election of 1824, no candidate achieved a majority. The Twelfth Amendment was used to decide the election. The results angered the followers of Jackson; therefore, Adams was able to do little as president.
2. Henry Clay wanted Adams to be chosen. He applied pressure on undecided House members to select Adams. Adams won the election, which angered Jackson.

Improvements to Transportation: Activity (p. 52)

Central Idea: Improvements were made to transportation in the early 1800s.

Road Details: a National Road built in 1811; first superhighway; privately owned turnpikes were built; conditions of roads were very poor

Canal Details: construction on the Erie Canal between Albany and Buffalo, New York, begins in 1817 and finishes in 1825; carried commerce of the Great Lakes to New York; made New York the center of the nation's trade; lowered the cost for shippers; other states built canals; canal era was short-lived due to the competition from railroads

Railroad Details: 1820s brought about steam engines; in 1828, construction begins on the B&O Railroad, other railroads followed; improvements to railroads came swiftly; railroads could transport people faster than stagecoaches; railroads in the North were superior to railroads in the South

Summary: Improvements were made to transportation in the early 1800s. A National Road was built in 1811. It served as the first superhighway. The Erie Canal was a huge success. It carried commerce of the Great Lakes to New York, making it the center of the nation's trade. Even though it lowered prices to shippers, it was short-lived due to the competition from railroads. The steam engine locomotive helped to make transportation by railroad possible. In 1828, construction began on the B&O Railroad. Other railroads followed, and improvements to railroads came swiftly. Railroads could transport people faster than stagecoaches. Railroads in the North were superior to railroads in the South.

The Five "Civilized" Tribes are Moved West: Activity (p. 54)

January 1825: Monroe requests creation of the Arkansas Territory and Indian Territory

1825: Chief William McIntosh signs a treaty giving up Creek tribal lands

April 1825: Chief McInosh killed for signing treaty

1826: Chief Menewa protests treaty in Washington, D.C.

1826: President Adams adds new clause to treaty that would cede less tribal land to Georgia

1829: Gold prospectors flood to Cherokee lands in northern Georgia

1830: President Jackson signs Indian Removal Act

1831: Choctaw travel from tribal lands to new homeland

1836: Chief Menewa leaves with Creek nation for Indian Territory

1836: Cherokee begin relocation to Indian Territory after President Jackson refuses to support Supreme Court ruling

October 1837: Chief Osceola of the Seminole captured

January 1838: Chief Osceola dies and followers surrender

1838: Remainder of Cherokee forced to leave tribal lands

Jackson Opposes the Central Banking System: Activity (p. 56)

(Answers will vary but may include:)

Activity One

Pros: made it easy for the government to borrow money; safe place to deposit money; could keep state banks from lending more money than they should to risky customers

Cons: too much power in the hands of the Bank president; board members were not kept informed of what was happening; Bank did not worry how fast loans to political figures were repaid; influenced newspaper coverage by buying ads in the newspapers

Activity Two

Action 1: vetoed the bill to recharter the Bank

Action 2: withdrew remaining government funds after paying bills

Action 3: removed tax money as soon as it was deposited and placed the money in state banks

The North Develops an Industrial Economy: Activity (p. 58)

(Answers will vary but may include:)

Early Textile Mills

Details: employed local workers; girls recruited from farms; girls lived in supervised boarding houses; worked 12-hour shifts; earned money; in bed by 9 P.M.; some laborers were children; lecturers brought in; tried to create a pleasant and moral atmosphere with flower boxes and sayings on machines

Factory Textile Mills

Details: new workers were immigrants from England, Ireland, or Europe; spoke little or no English; girls had little education; required to work long hours; factory owners more interested in making money than caring for workers; mills were dirty and noisy; mills were hot in the summer and cold in winter; some workers developed lung diseases from inhaling lint particles

Summary: In early textile mills, workers were recruited from the local area or surrounding farms. Girls lived in supervised boarding houses. They worked a 12-hour shift and were in bed by 9 P.M. The mill owners cared about the workers and tried to provide a pleasant and moral atmosphere. Factory mill owners cared more about making money than caring for workers. New workers were immigrants from England, Ireland, or Europe. They spoke little or no English. The factory mills were dirty and noisy. They were hot in the summer and cold in winter. Some workers developed lung diseases from inhaling lint particles.

Sam Houston Leads Texans to Independence: Activity (p. 60)

(Teacher verification is required.)

The Oregon Territory: Activity (p. 62)

The Fur Trade

Key Details: Robert Gray traveled to Pacific Northwest in 1787 seeking sea-otter furs to trade with China; 1792 discovered Columbia River, discovery allowed U.S. claim to Oregon territory; John Jacob Astor established Fort Astoria in Oregon for fur trade; Hudson Bay Company in 1821 was still a presence in fur trade in Oregon.

Interest in Annexation and Settlement

Key Details: Congressman John Floyd wanted to annex Oregon; people felt Oregon was too far away and Rocky Mountains was natural boundary to the U.S.

Missionaries

Key Details: missionaries interested in converting Native Americans to Christianity; missionaries Whitman and Spalding brought their wives, shattering belief the journey was too hard on women

Oregon Trail

Key Details: 1840s, high interest in going to Oregon for free land, sense of adventure, desire to make Oregon part of the U.S.; in 1843, a wagon train left Independence with 1,000 people; successful overland journey depended on listening to good leaders, good team of oxen, horses, or mules and a sturdy wagon; and traveling light

Summary: Before Lewis and Clark reached Oregon, American Robert Gray had already traveled to the Pacific Northwest. In 1787, he went there to seek sea-otter furs to trade with China. In 1792, he discovered the Columbia River. This discovery allowed the U.S. to lay claim to Oregon territory. The fur trade increased when John Jacob Astor established Fort Astoria in Oregon. Hudson Bay Company in 1821 was still a presence in fur trade in Oregon. Congressman John Floyd wanted to annex Oregon, but most people felt Oregon was too far away and the Rocky Mountains was the natural boundary to the U.S. Later, missionaries traveled to the area. They were interested in converting Native Americans to Christianity. Missionaries Whitman and Spalding brought their wives on their journey to Oregon. This shattered the belief that the journey was too hard on women. People flocked to Oregon in the 1840s looking for free land, a sense of adventure, and the desire to make Oregon part of the U.S. In 1843, a wagon train left Independence with 1,000 people. A successful journey depended on people listening to good leaders; having a good team of oxen, horses, or mules and a sturdy wagon; and traveling light.

The Reform Movement in Pre-Civil War America: Activity (p. 64)

1. The movement called for limiting the use of or abstaining from alcohol.
2. He pushed for tax-supported public education.
3. She brought about better treatment for the mentally ill.

4. She was America's first female physician.
5. It was a Utopian community.
6. A religious group who were the first critics of slavery
7. He was a free African American who co-owned and published the first African-American-owned newspaper, *Freedom's Journal.*
8. He was a free African American who co-owned and published the first African-American-owned newspaper, *Freedom's Journal.*
9. A Quaker, he published *The Genius of Universal Emancipation.*
10. An assistant to Benjamin Lundy, he thought the Quaker approach was too slow and called for the immediate freeing of slaves. He started a newspaper, *The Liberator.*
11. He was the abolitionist editor of the *Alton Observer* in Illinois. He was murdered by a pro-slavery mob for advocating the formation of an anti-slavery society.

Nicholas Trist and the Mexican-American War: Activity (p. 66)

1. At first, Trist and Scott did not get along. Scott felt Trist was sent by President Polk to spy on him. When Trist got sick on the trip, Scott felt sorry for Trist and gave him a jar of jam. After this, the relationship improved.
2. The terms of the treaty were Mexico gave up any claim to Texas, ceded Upper California and New Mexico to the United States in exchange for $15 million, and established the Texas boundary at the Rio Grande.
3. Trist received orders from the president to return home. He consulted with Scott, who felt Trist should stay and finish negotiations. Trist defied orders and remained. Since the treaty was good, Polk accepted the terms, but he got even with Trist. He fired Trist when he returned home and refused to pay his salary and accrued expenses.

The California Gold Rush: Activity (p. 68)

History of California: Early settlements were scattered, with only a few missions, ranches, and towns in the territory. Native Americans were thought of as cheap labor. Americans in California before 1840 were fur trappers, whalers, and cattle buyers. To get to California, most traveled by sea around South America.

Early American Settlers: Early American settlers were Thomas Larkin, a merchant in Monterrey, and ranchers, John Marsh and Johann Sutter.

Overland Trail: Overland travel was difficult. Lansford Hastings wrote a book, called *The Emigrant's Guide to California.* The famous Donner Party took an unexplored cutoff mentioned in the book and were stranded in the Sierra Nevadas.

Gold Is Discovered: When California became a territory of the U.S., a large part of the population was Mexican. This changed when gold was discovered, and Americans flocked to California.

The Gold Rush: In 1849, thousands of men flocked to California. They traveled overland; sailed down to Panama, crossed the narrow country, and then sailed up to California; or came by ship around South America. Few struck the "big bonanza."

The Compromise of 1850: Activity (p. 70)

(Answers will vary but may include:)

The map shows the Missouri Compromise of 1820 line and the Mason and Dixon line. It also shows which states and territories are free, which are slave states, and the territories where slavery was determined by popular sovereignty.

"Bleeding Kansas": Activity (p. 72)

(Answers will vary but may include:)

<u>Expansion of the Railroads</u>

Details: need for expansion caused by rapid growth of California; interest in building transcontinental railroad; railroads needed a customer base, so Kansas territory needed to be surveyed

<u>Kansas-Nebraska Act</u>

Details: proposed by Stephen Douglas; formed Kansas and Nebraska territories and allowed settlers to decide whether to be slave or free; Southerners backed the act, Northerners opposed the act

<u>Northerners and Southerners Flock to Kansas</u>

Details: North and South wanted to get control of Kansas, so population increased from both sides; election was held resulting in pro-slavery legislature set up at Lecompton and anti-slavery legislature at Topeka

<u>Acts of Violence</u>

Details: Horace Greeley used term "Bleeding Kansas"; Lawrence attacked by border ruffians; John Brown led attack on pro-slavery town, Pottawatomie Creek

John Brown Attacks Harpers Ferry: Activity (p. 74)

Headline: (Answers will vary.)

Byline: (Answers will vary.)

Who: John Brown

What: led a raid on Harpers Ferry

When: October 16, 1859

Where: Harpers Ferry, Virginia.

Why: planned to arm slaves, which would signal a general slave rebellion

How: Brown and his slave army would flee to the mountains, where they would fight off their enemies, until all slaves were free.

Other Facts or Details: (Answers will vary.)

John Brown was a man of action, more than words; Virginia was a slave state; Harpers Ferry had a federal arsenal, armory, and rifle works; Boston abolitionists, known as the Secret Six, gave Brown $10,000 for his venture; Colonel Robert E. Lee was sent to Harpers Ferry with some marines; Brown turned down an offer to surrender; Brown was captured; ten of his men were killed, including two of his sons.

South Carolina Secedes: Activity (p. 76)

1. The Democratic Convention met in Charleston, South Carolina, in April. They did not select any candidates. The Party met again in Baltimore. The Southern delegates walked out and chose Senator John Breckinridge of Kentucky as their candidate. The Northern delegates chose Senator Stephen Douglas of Illinois.
2. The Republican Convention met in Chicago. Abraham Lincoln was selected as the candidate on the third ballot. Their platform promised homesteads, a railroad to the Pacific, and tariff protection for American industries. On the issue of slavery, the platform opposed interference with slavery in the states.
3. Douglas urged the South to stay in the Union, regardless of how the election turned out.
4. South Carolina legislature called for a convention to discuss secession. Six other states decided to hold secession conventions. After the conventions, all seven states voted to leave the Union. They held a meeting in Montgomery, Alabama, and formed the Confederate States of America. Jefferson Davis was elected as provisional president.

Lincoln Asks for 75,000 Volunteers: Activity (p. 78)

(Answers will vary but may include:)

1. The states of South Carolina, Georgia, Alabama, Florida, Mississippi, Louisiana, and Texas have opposed the laws of the United States and their execution by the United States in such a huge way that it can't be handled by the judicial system.
2. I, Abraham Lincoln, by the powers given to me by the Constitution, call for 75,000 men from the state militias to help execute the laws of the land. The details will be conveyed to the states by the War Department.
3. I ask all citizens to agree with and support this effort to preserve the Union.
4. The first assignment of the militia will be to repossess the forts, places, and property that rightfully belong to the Union. We will try to do this without any damage or destruction to the property of loyal citizens.

African Americans and the War Effort: Activity (p. 80)

1. F	2. F	3. T	4. T	5. F
6. T	7. T	8. T	9. F	10. T
11. T	12. F	13. F	14. T	15. T

A Time of Southern Victories: Activity (p. 82)

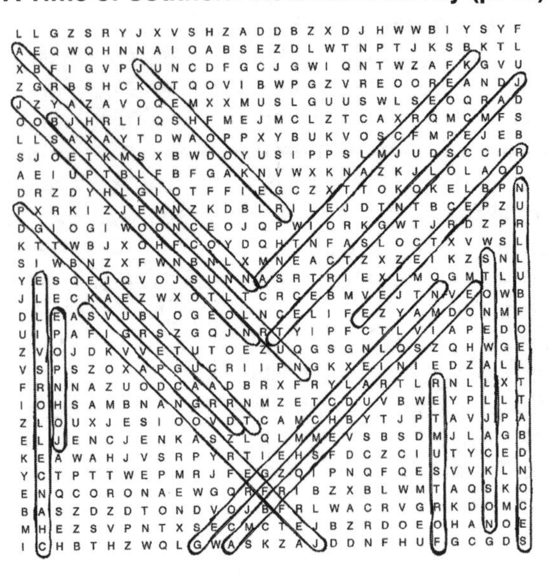

July 4, 1863—A Day of Northern Victories: Activity (p. 84)

1. If Vicksburg fell, it would divide the western and eastern parts of the Confederacy.
2. General Lee hoped to relieve pressure on Vicksburg by forcing Grant to send Northern army troops after him. He hoped it would encourage peace talks with the North, and he would feed his army at the North's expense.
3. (Answers will vary.)
4. If General Meade would have captured Lee and his troops, it would have probably ended the war. As a result, the war continued for two more years.

Women Join the War Effort on Both Sides: Activity (p. 86)

<u>Women on the Home Front</u>

Main Idea: During the war, women supported the home front.

Details: took over the running of farms; went to work in factories to produce arms and clothing

<u>Women Spies</u>

Main Idea: Women on both sides served as spies during the Civil War.

Details: reported on troop movements; were imprisoned, sometimes multiple times; some women pretended to be men and enlisted in the army

<u>Women Serve as Nurses</u>

Main Idea: Women served as nurses during the Civil War.

Details: homes were opened to sick and wounded soldiers; cooked meals and treated wounds; Dorothea Dix served as Superintendent of United States Army nurses; Clara Barton, a Civil War nurse, was the founder of the American Red Cross

President Lincoln Is Assassinated: Activity (p. 88)

(Teacher verification is required.)